Word Processing
Lew Hollerbach

Second edition

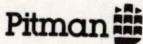

PITMAN PUBLISHING
128 Long Acre, London WC2E 9AN

A Division of Longman Group UK Limited

© Lew Hollerbach 1983

First published in Great Britain 1983
by arrangement with the Orlando Press, Bath
Reprinted 1984 (twice), 1985
Second edition 1986
Reprinted 1987, 1988, 1991 (twice)

British Library Cataloguing in Publication Data
Hollerbach, Lew
 Word processing. —2nd ed. —(Pitman
 office guide)
 1. Word processing
 652'.5   HF5548.115

All rights reserved. No part of this publication may be reproduced, stored in a retrieval system, or transmitted in any form or by any means, electronic, mechanical, photocopying, recording, or otherwise without either the prior written permission of the Publishers or a licence permitting restricted copying in the United Kingdom issued by the Copyright Licensing Agency Ltd, 90 Tottenham Court Road, London, W1P 9HE. This book may not be lent, resold, hired out or otherwise disposed of by way of trade in any form of binding or cover other than that in which it is published without the prior consent of the Publishers.

Technical illustrations: John Bowering

Produced by Longman Group (FE) Ltd
Printed in Hong Kong

ISBN 0273 02511 2

Contents

1 **Introducing word processing** 1
   The usefulness of a word processor 1
   The language of word processing 4
   Some common uses 4

2 **The building blocks of a word processor** 8
   Introduction 9
      Memory 9
      The microprocessor 10
      Software 10
   The screen and keyboard 11
      Characteristics of screens 12
      Keyboards 12
   Disks 16
      Floppy disks 17
      Hard disks 18
   Printers and stationery 19
      Daisywheel printers 20
      Dot matrix printers 23
      Laser printers 23
      Ink-jet printers 24
      Thermal printers 24
      Paper-handling 24
      Ribbons 24
      Stationery 25
   Communications 26
      Standards 27

3 **A session at the word processor** 31
   The principal features 31
      Text entry 31
      Storage 36
      Printing 41
      Editing 46
   A few extras 51
      Spelling dictionary 51
      Foreign languages, symbols and line graphics 52

iii

    Calculator   54
    List processing   55
    Records management   56
    User programming   59
    Integration   61
    Mouse   62
    Windows   63

4 Questions and answers   64
Analyzing the needs   64
Recognizing the solutions   66
    Choices   66
    Configurations   68
    Financing   71
    Bureaux   73

5 Evaluating systems   75
The hardware   75
The software   77
The supplier   78
    The sales pitch   79
    Demonstrations   79
    Agreements   81

6 Implementation   82
Installation   82
Training   82
    By your supplier   83
    By an outside organization   83
    Teach-yourself   83
Use   84
    The care of the word processor   84
    The care of disks   84
    Hints and tips   85
    If something goes wrong   87
Preserving the investment   89
    Insurance   89
    Maintenance contracts   90

7 Glossary   91

1 Introducing word processing

The usefulness of a word processor

What is a word processor? It is a machine — a computer, in fact — which allows you to work with letters, words, paragraphs and documents.

In this book, the term 'word processor' covers both kinds of machine: the **dedicated** word processor, which is used only for word processing, and a general-purpose personal computer used for word processing among other uses. (For a comparison of dedicated and general-purpose computers, see Chapter 4.)

A word processor is not just an advanced typewriter. Although both word processors and typewriters allow creation and printing of text, the word processor has two important distinguishing features:

- text can be stored for future use — if you need to work with it again, it doesn't have to be retyped;
- text can be corrected, modified and rearranged before committing it to paper, without retyping it.

Here are some more special qualities of a word processor:

- It consists mostly of electronic circuitry, and has few moving parts.
- It is very much faster than a typewriter (or any mechanical device) and more reliable.
- It gives the operator total control and flexibility in manipulating text.
- It is very compact, considering the amount of work it can do and the ease with which it does it.

Here is how the word processor handles text. Compare this with the way a typewriter works.

Introducing word processing 1

- Text is typed at a keyboard, but doesn't appear on paper; instead, it is displayed on a TV-like screen, and electronically filed by the word processor.

- If the text needs changes — correction of spelling mistakes, inserting or removing paragraphs — *only these changes* are typed. What is correct is untouched and does not need retyping. The correction, rearrangement and other modification of text are called **editing**.)

- Only when the text is perfect does it finally appear on paper. Also, since the text has been filed, it can be printed as many times as needed, without retyping or photocopying.

There is much to be gained by using a word processor.

- Productivity is substantially increased. No longer is time wasted for the sake of editing. As a bonus, typing speed is improved. More time is also available for typing new text, since editing is so much easier.

- Composition of text is simplified: many facilities are available to control text layout — page lengths, margins, and position of text can all be specified (and changed when needed) by the operator.

- Better quality of text is produced: again, there are many facilities available to define the appearance of text on paper. Different styles of type, automatic centering of headings, newspaper-style columns are a few examples.

Word processors are popular and in widespread use because:

- many time-consuming manual tasks have been automated;
- tasks that previously took an excessively long time are now done quickly.

General office uses

- The most frequent application of word processors is for typing *general correspondence* (letters, memos, etc.), where the ability to correct and change text easily is the main benefit. Spelling mistakes can be caught on the screen, before printing, and

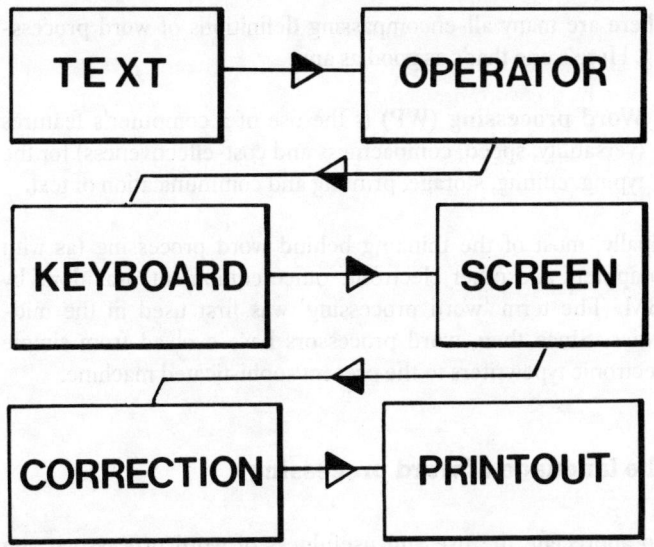

How the word processor is used

words and sentences can be added or deleted without retyping the whole text.

- *Reports*, which are often long, and undergo a lot of revision, are well-suited for word processors. Not only is it easy to add, change or delete text; you can also use the word processor to help you with the organization and layout of the report. Margins can be easily set (or reset to a different measure), headings or footings inserted and page numbers automatically added, to name just a few features. A spelling dictionary can be helpful for technical reports, and the search-and-replace feature can correct recurring mistakes.

- *Personalized letters*: if you need to send circulars, reminders or other standard text to a large number of people (e.g. in a mail-order campaign, or to all your clients), the word processor is of great help. You only need to key in the letter once; all you do then is add a name and address — possibly a salutation — print the letter, insert the next name, print the next letter, and so on.

- repetitive tasks that wasted human resources are now done efficiently, automatically.

Introducing word processing 3

There are many all-encompassing definitions of word processing. Here's one that's as good as any:

- **Word processing (WP)** is the use of a computer's features (versatility, speed, compactness and cost-effectiveness) for the typing, editing, storage, printing and communication of text.

Finally, most of the thinking behind word processing (as with computers and other electronic office equipment) was done by IBM. The term 'word processing' was first used in the midsixties. Since then, word processors have evolved from simple electronic typewriters to the present sophisticated machine.

The language of word processing

To appreciate the use and usefulness of word processors, you must have an understanding of what they do and how they work. You must know the language in which the relevant information is expressed. A lot of this language is jargon.

- Many words are familiar, because the concepts behind them have parallels in non-word processing; for example, many of the terms are the same as in the printing and publishing industries.

- Many of the words are commonly used ones, but have taken on a new meaning.

- Some words are artificial, created by leading companies in the word processing and computer industry.

- There are abbreviations and acronyms (words formed from the first letters, or first few letters, of several other words). Abbreviations and acronyms are useful — they can be used as a shorthand in writing and speaking.

Jargon words aren't a problem once you get used to them.

Some common uses

Although a word processor is often seen as a typewriter replacement, there are many uses to which it can be put in addition to typing. Here are a few of the most common ones, in which some of the special facilities of the word processor are put to use.

- Alternatively, you can key in the letter and save it, and have the word processor automatically merge a name-and-address list with the letter, during which the word processor prints out a copy of the letter correctly addressed to each name on the list.

- Such a list-processing option would also let you add or delete names, select from a list of names (e.g. according to region or profession), and print labels.

Legal and financial uses

- In legal work, typing *contracts* takes up a lot of time. With a word processor, you need key in only once all the clauses you would ever use, give each a name or number, and save them on disk. When you need a contract, all you do is specify (in order) the name or number of the clauses you need, and the word processor will automatically retrieve them from the disk, and assemble them into a document, appropriately numbered. You can then make any changes before printing the final contract.

- In financial work, you'll be dealing with rows and columns of *numbers*, such as those found in balance sheets and other financial reports. Using any line graphics facilities will enhance the appearance of the report — the columns can be separated by vertical lines, and other figures can be highlighted by putting boxes round them.

- The decimal tab key can help you with keying a column of figures, by lining up the decimal points, and a built-in calculator lets you double-check all rows and column totals and percentages.

- On some word processors, this mathematical mode has been greatly extended. If for example you are entering figures on a balance sheet, or editing a balance sheet, you can enter (or amend) the figures in the columns, and let the machine take care of adding up the totals correctly. If you are word processing on a general-purpose computer, you have a lot more scope for using mathematical and financial calculations.

- If you regularly have to write out documents using a standard layout, for example company accounts, where each page has a different layout, you can get the machine to 'read across' from another document (e.g. the profit-and-loss account) and it will bring up the layout you require, with tabs, margins etc. as appropriate.

Scientific and engineering uses

Most scientific and engineering use consists of *reports*, *theses* and *dissertations*. Usually these include equations, formulae and tables.

- The word processor's ability to handle *special symbols*, *subscripts* and *superscripts* is of great benefit. An abbreviation dictionary may help: you may type *equ* instead of *equation*; the word processor will find every occurrence of the abbreviation and substitute the full word. Spelling dictionaries can also be useful for technical terms.

- *Tables of data* are easily handled — the decimal tab key is used to line up columns of numbers; line graphics features let you put neat boxes around the tables, and headings can easily be centred.

- Word processors can have a *keystroke memory*, i.e. they are able to remember specified sequences of keystrokes. You may for example regularly use a certain sequence of figures, or a certain rectangular shape. You can call these up without having to key the whole sequence each time.

Summary of benefits offered by the word processor

- mistakes can be easily corrected;
  texts can be stored for re-use (cutting out repetitive word);
  layouts can be re-arranged without having to write out the text again;
  using a word processor is physically less tiring than using a typewriter;
  the final appearance of WP texts is high-class;
  word processors save time;
  word processors can assemble material from different places;
  word processors can help people with spelling.

All these features add up to

- greater productivity;
  greater accuracy;
  speedier and better-looking output;
  less boredom for the operator.

2 The building blocks of a word processor

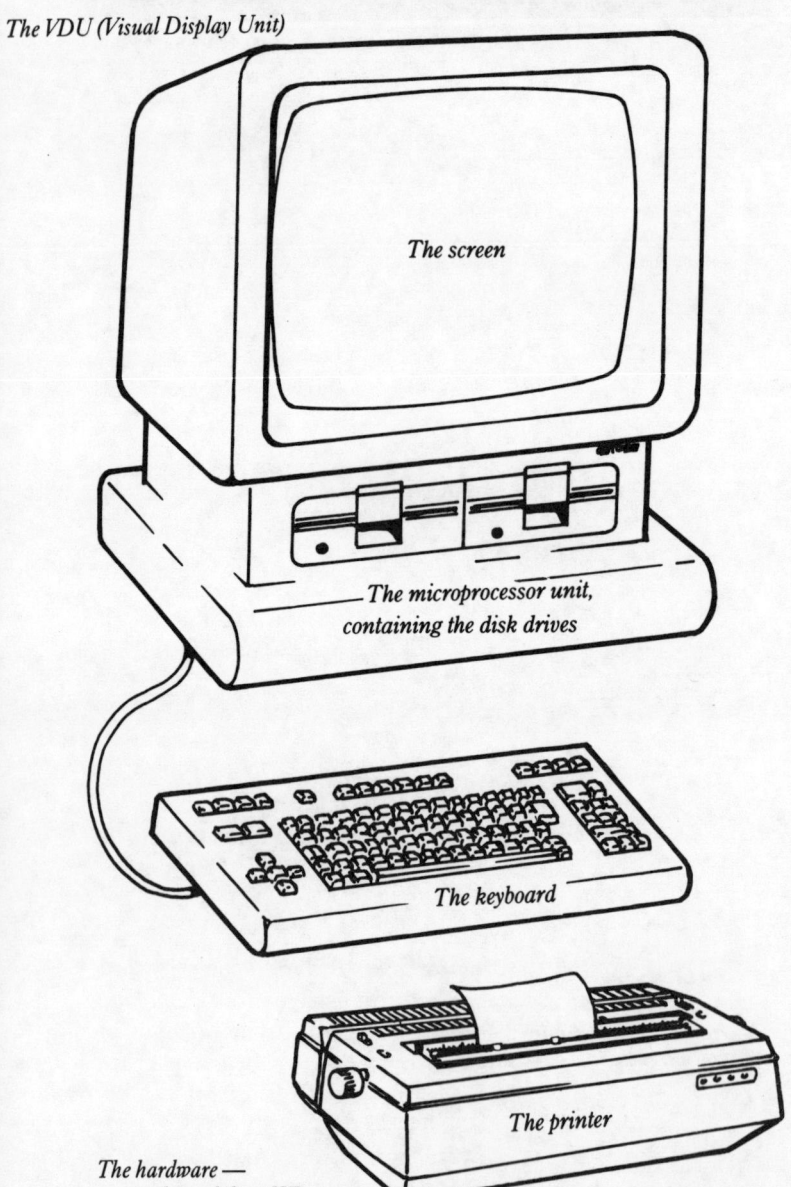

The VDU (Visual Display Unit)

The screen

The microprocessor unit, containing the disk drives

The keyboard

The printer

The hardware — a typical standalone WP system

8 Word Processing

Introduction

A word processor is a computer. A dedicated word processor and a computer which has word processing software look similar. They have four components:

- a TV-like screen;
- a typewriter-style keyboard;
- a printer;
- a set of disk units.

Word processors are often called word processing systems.

- A **system** is a group of separate components (keyboard, screen, etc.) connected together to function as a unit (word processor).

The generic term for the components is **hardware**. A word processor is also often called a **workstation**.

What you can't see when looking at a word processor is the electronics that make it work. They're contained in the case that holds the screen.

There are two important parts to the electronics that you should know about: memory and the microprocessor.

Memory

- In order to display and edit the text, it must be held somewhere. **Memory** is a temporary storage for text. Its capacity is expressed as the number of characters (letters, numbers and symbols) it can hold.

- You may come across the term *byte* when looking at word processors. **Byte** is a computer term, used to measure storage capacity. On a word processor, one byte is the amount of memory needed to hold one character; hence, bytes and characters are identical units of measurement of memory.

- Memory in a word processor is large, and the byte is not a convenient unit to work with. Therefore, a **kilobyte** is used, abbreviated to **K**. A kilobyte is 1024 bytes; hence 48K is 49,152 bytes.

- Despite the size of the memory, not all of it is available for storing text. The part of memory assigned to text storage is often called a **buffer**.

- Memory is temporary storage — as soon as power is turned off, its contents disappear. You will see later that a more permanent means of storage is used, in the form of disks.

The microprocessor

The **microprocessor** controls the whole operation of a word processor. It is a versatile and inexpensive device, found not only in word processors, but in all small computers, washing machines, traffic lights, and so forth.

In a word processor, the microprocessor is responsible for:
- accepting text from the keyboard, and storing it in memory;
- displaying text on the screen;
- accepting commands from the operator and carrying them out;
- arranging the text to be printed;
- controlling the operation of the printer and disks.

If the microprocessor is such a versatile device that it can be used in many diverse pieces of equipment, how does it 'know' what to do when used in a word processor?

Software

The microprocessor is so adaptable because it can follow instructions. All activities in word processing can be expressed in a formal manner, as a series of steps to be taken by the microprocessor. For example, to display a character on the screen, the microprocessor must scan the keyboard, determine what key has been pressed, create the required character, direct the electronics of the screen to display it, and also put it into memory.

At the most elementary level, this formalism is reduced to patterns of electronic signals to which the microprocessor can react.

- **Software** is the generic name given to sets of instructions that can be acted on by the microprocessor.

- It is 'soft' because you can't see or feel it — only experience its effects or consequences.

- Software must also be held in memory in order for the microprocessor to act on it. The largest proportion of memory is devoted to storing software.

- It is through software that a microprocessor controls the operation of the word processor. Remember that, in its lowest form, software is a set of electronic signals that has a fixed meaning to the microprocessor, enabling it to control other electronic circuitry.

Finally, remember that software is an integral part of the word processing system. On its own, it can do nothing, and hardware without it is also useless.

The screen and keyboard

The main activity of word processing, that of keying text, is done using a keyboard. A **keyboard** is a collection of switches, each representing a character or action to be taken. When a key is pressed, the action is performed, or the character is displayed on the screen.

The **screen** replaces paper in the traditional typewriter. It is technically the same as a TV screen but instead of displaying pictures, it displays text.

The combination of screen and keyboard is sometimes given the name **VDU** (Visual Display Unit). The screen may be called by its proper technical name **CRT** (Cathode Ray Tube).

Consider some of the features of this screen/keyboard combination that make it so common and convenient for word processing:

- It is easy to enter and manipulate text with a keyboard — all you do is press the required keys. Entering text is often called **keying**.

- As you press a key (a **keystroke**) you can always see the results of that keystroke — a character is displayed or an action is performed.

- You can receive messages on the screen. If, for example, you tried to do something that is not possible, a message will appear telling you so.

- The screen is silent and very fast in operation. It's easy to display new text, change it, clear the screen, as often as needed. There is no noise, and no resources such as paper are wasted.

- The screen and keyboard are reliable devices. The only moving parts are the key switches. If treated properly, they last a very long time.

Remember that the screen is a two-way device — it will always show you what you've entered, and the results of any actions you've specified.

Characteristics of screens

All screens have certain specifications that are given in WP brochures. These are:

- **character set** — the number of letters, numbers and other symbols that can be displayed (this is also related to the keyboard).

- **character formation** — if you look closely at a character on the screen, you will see that it is made up of a number of tiny dots of light, arranged in a grid. Character formation refers to the number of rows and columns in the grid. This grid is called a **matrix**.

- **display format** — either the total number of characters that can be displayed on the screen, or the number of lines and characters within a line that can be displayed (multiply the lines by the characters in the line to give total that will fit on the screen). You'll often see page display and part-page display being used.

- **page display** — the screen can display between 50 and 70 lines, with 80 characters in line. Page displays contain the same number of characters that would be found in a standard A4 page.

- **part-page display** — this is the most common type of display, and means that the screen can show between 16 and 24 lines, with 80 characters in a line.

A point to watch for when choosing a system is how much the on-screen text resembles the final printed version. With some word processors, you have a facility for 'viewing' the text as it will appear on paper, although you can't enter or edit text in this mode.

A word processor which shows the text on screen exactly as it will look on paper is called **WYSIWYG** — What You See Is What You Get.

The colour of the background and characters is also given. Here are a few possibilities:

- black (or dark green) background, with white, light green, blue or bronze (orange) characters. These are the most prevalent combinations.

- white background with black characters. With this combination, the screen is supposed to resemble a piece of paper (since screens replace paper, you may wonder why some manufacturers chose this; nevertheless, some people like it).

Other characteristics may be given, such as the size of the characters displayed, and the size of the screen, measured diagonally, in inches or centimetres.

All screens will have some means of reducing stray reflections, and will have a brightness control. Some screens will allow you to tilt them up or down, and swivel them from side to side.

You'll hear the word *cursor* being used in connection with word processing screens.

- A **cursor** is an indicator to the operator, showing where text is to be entered.

- As a key is pressed, a character appears, and the cursor moves along one position to the right.

- The cursor can be moved to any position on the screen, in any direction.

- It can take on several forms: stationary or flashing, solid rectangle or underline, for example.

Keyboards

With few exceptions, keyboard layouts are identical to that of a typewriter, as far as the positioning of the text keys is concerned. This layout is called **QWERTY**, referring to the first six keys on the left-hand side of the second row.

The QWERTY layout is now the international standard, although the French use an AZERTY keyboard.

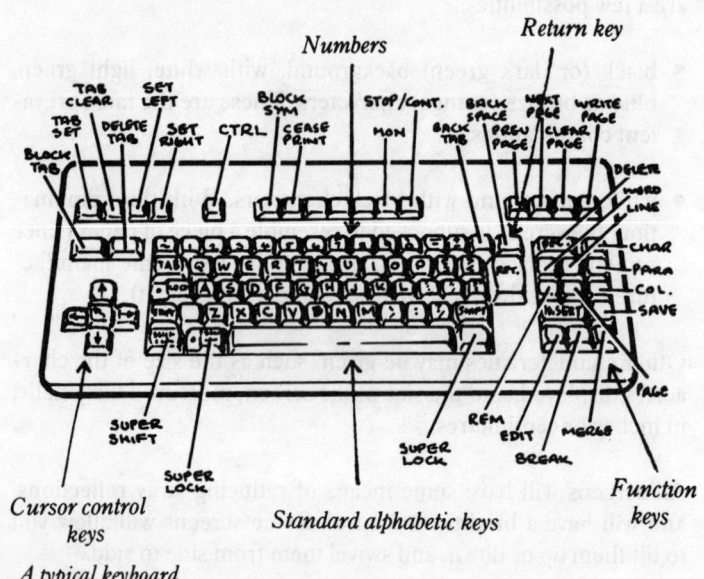

A typical keyboard

In addition to the letter keys, you'll see the following:

- a row of number keys, and above the numbers, symbols such as @, &, ", ';

- the SHIFT keys, which display capitals and the above symbols;

- several keys with other symbols on them, such as , . ; ? ;

- a TAB key, which is used to position the cursor at a certain location within a line without repeatedly pressing the space bar;

14 Word Processing

- a BACKSPACE key (often labelled with a ◊), which allows you to correct simple spelling mistakes, by moving the cursor back to the mistake;

- a CAPS LOCK key, which allows capitals and numbers to be displayed without SHIFTing;

- four or five CURSOR CONTROL keys, each key having an arrow on it showing the direction of the cursor when the key is pressed. The possible movements are: up, down, left, right. The optional fifth key moves the cursor to the top left corner of the screen;

- the RETURN or CARRIAGE RETURN key. Often, this just labelled with an arrow (⏎). This key is used to mark the end of a section of text, such as a paragraph, for example. It is so called because it makes the cursor jump to the left of the screen, and on to a new line, like the return on a typewriter.

There are still more keys, called **function keys**, which are used for the editing and other functions of the word processor. The names of these keys, their location, and their purpose depends on the machine.

Generally, there are two ways in which functions can be carried out — with dedicated keys, or using mnemonics.

- With **dedicated** keys, each editing function — in fact, virtually every function the word processor can carry out — is assigned its own key.

- Using **mnemonics** reduces the number of keys on the keyboard. Instead of each key being assigned a unique function, only a small number of keys are used, in conjunction with some of the text keys. For example, to remove a word from a line, you might press a key with a screen symbol on it, followed by R (for *remove*) and W (for *word*).

All keyboards have an **automatic repeat** facility. This means that if a key is held down long enough (half a second), the character will be repeated automatically, until the key is released. Cursor control keys also have automatic repeat.

Since keyboards do not make any noise when a key is pressed, some manufacturers build in an audible 'beep' to signal a keystroke. The intensity of the beep can be varied. Finally, most keyboards are detachable, which means they can be moved around to suit individual preferences.

Disks

A **disk** is a device that holds a large amount of text in a more permanent way. The amount of storage on a disk is also expressed in K, or **M** (**megabytes**; a megabyte is 1000K, i.e., 1,024,000 bytes).

Disks are essential in word processing because:

- the word processor's memory is not suitable for permanent storage, since its contents disappear when the power supply is turned off;
- much more can be stored on a disk than can be held in memory.

The term *disk* or *diskette* refers to the medium, and the hardware that makes it work is called a **disk drive**. Disks are classified as:

- floppy or hard;
- fixed or exchangeable.
- **Floppies** are so called because they consist of a flexible plastic disk enclosed in a rigid square plastic envelope. Floppies are always exchangeable.
- **Hard disks**, as the name implies, are made of aluminium. Hard disks may be fixed or exchangeable.
- **Fixed disks** cannot be removed from the disk drive; therefore, one disk stores all the text.
- **Exchangeable disks** can be removed, so many disks can be used to store text.

Text is stored on disks in the same way as music is stored on audio cassettes. The surface of the disk is coated with a magnetic compound, and electrical signals representing the text are fed on to the surface using an electromagnet.

There are two main disk specifications you need to know about: size and capacity.

- **Size** — diameter of the disk in inches or millimetres (mm).
- **Capacity** — (K or M) the space available for storing text.

Floppy disks

Floppy disks come in two standard sizes: 8" (203mm) and 5¼" (133mm). A smaller, more recent size is the **micro disk**, which comes enclosed in a plastic case, and varies between 3" and 3½" (75–89mm).

Floppies can also be:

- **single-sided** — only one side used for storage;
- **double-sided** — both sides used for storage;
- **single-density**;
- **double-density** — roughly double the capacity of single-sided disks;
- single-sided, single-density;
- double-sided, single-density;
- double-sided, single-density;
- double-sided, double-density.

Single-density floppies are sometimes called *single-tracking*, and

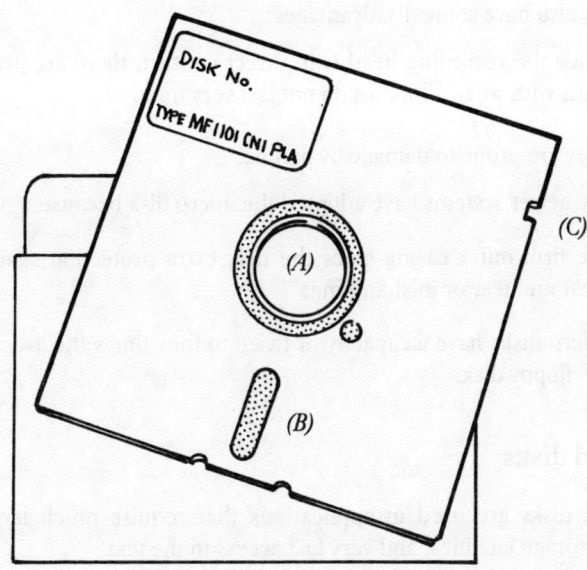

The building blocks of a word processor 17

double-density are called *double-tracking*. The type of floppy used on a word processor depends on its manufacturer.

The amount of data a disk will hold is its **capacity**. The capacity of floppy and micro disks currently varies between 140K and 720K.

There are two cut-outs in the envelope, one circular in the middle (A), the other oblong, to one side (B). The disk is rotated by a clamp which grips it in the middle through the circular hub. The recording head moves along the oblong slot to store and recall text.

There is also a little notch (C), which, when covered, will prevent anything being stored on the disk. This is useful for protecting valuable text from inadvertent over-recording.

Floppies have many advantages, and almost all word processors use them.

- Disks are cheap and easy to store because of their small size.
- They are removable — as many disks as needed can be used for storage.
- Double-sided, double-density disks provide large storage capacities.

They also have some disadvantages:

- since the recording head is in direct contact, there are problems with wear. Floppies do not last very long;
- they are prone to damage by people.

Many newer systems have adopted the micro disk because:

- the firm outer casing gives the disk extra protection against wear and tear or mishandling;
- micro disks have a capacity of twice to four times the average $5\frac{3}{4}''$ floppy disk.

Hard disks

Hard disks are used in applications that require much larger text storage facilities, and very fast access to the text.

A popular type of exchangeable hard disk is the **cartridge disk**.

- A cartridge disk is so-called because it is contained in a large, round, strong plastic case, or cartridge.

- It is similar to a floppy, but has a much greater storage capacity, and storage capacities vary from 10M to around 20M.

Hard disks are often found as a fixed–exchangeable combination.

- The disk drive holds two disks — one at the bottom of the drive, one at the top.

- The bottom disk is fixed — it can't be removed. The top disk, being the actual cartridge, can be removed.

- The top disk is used to store copies of text held on the bottom disk. This facility gives a measure of security, should the bottom disk break down.

- Hard disks and their drives are rather bulky, and need a lot of room.

How the hard disk works:

- The disk is hermetically sealed in its disk drive, so no dust can get in.

- The disk rotates at high speed, and the recording head floats a tiny distance above the disk, supported on a cushion of air.

The advantages of a hard disk are:

- it is fast and compact — large amounts of text can be stored and retrieved very quickly;

- since there is no contact between head and disk, there are no wear problems, and hence a longer life and a tenfold improvement in reliability.

When using a hard disk, you may need to make backup copies on floppy disks or magnetic tape. A number of floppies are needed for each hard disk.

Printers and stationery

A **printer** prints text created by a word processor on to paper.

The building blocks of a word processor 19

All printers have certain characteristics which you should be familiar with. These are:

- **Speed** — number of characters printed per second (**CPS**).
- **Paper handling** — maximum width of paper that can be accommodated; given in inches or centimetres, or in terms of A and B sizes.
- **Printing density** — also called **pitch**, this is the number of characters printed per horizontal inch.
- **Print element** — daisywheel or dot matrix.
- **Character set** — as with screen and keyboard, the number of characters that can be printed.

Printers used with word processors are much like typewriters:

- they rely on a mechanical force to transfer the character on to paper, and are used in conjunction with a ribbon.

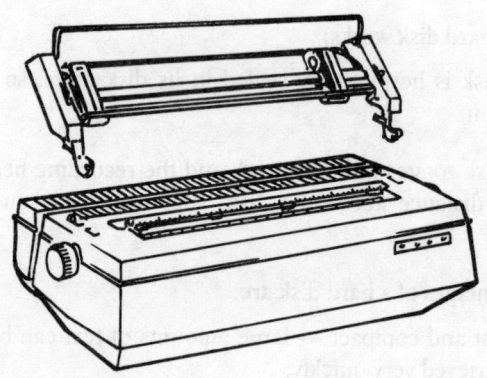

A printer, with tractor feed

Daisywheel printers

Daisywheel printers are so called because:

- they use a round printwheel, with the characters at the end of *petals*;
- the wheel rotates until the required character is in position, for a hammer to fly out and hit it, transferring the character on to a ribbon, and paper.

20 Word Processing

Daisywheel printers are sometimes called *letter-quality*, or *correspondence-quality*, because of their high quality of printing.

Daisywheels themselves are made of plastic or metal, and are available in pica, elite, or proportional pitch.

- **Pica** — 10 pitch, or 10 characters printed per horizontal inch.
- **Elite** — 12 pitch, or 12 characters per inch.
- 15 pitch is also available.
- Pica and elite are examples of **monospacing**, in which a fixed amount of space is taken up irrespective of the character.
- In **proportional** pitch, each character takes up only the space it needs; for example, the letter *i* needs less space than *m*.
- Text printed in proportional pitch looks more 'professional'.
- Plastic daisywheels usually have 96 characters on them, and are available in 10, 12 or 15 pitch.
- Metal daisywheels have 88, 92 or 96 characters, and allow proportional printing.

Typical features of daisywheel printers include:

- Speeds — 15–55 CPS.
- Varieties of **typefaces**, or **fonts**, available, for different styles of printing (e.g. Roman or *italic*) foreign languages, mathematical symbols, which mean only selecting the appropriate wheel.
- **Bidirectional printing** — this means that the printing head prints both when moving to the right and on the return trip.
- **Logic-seeking** — in essence, this means that the printer will not 'print' blank spaces, which results in faster printing.
- Selectable line spacing — half-space, single-space, $1\frac{1}{2}$ space, double-space; half-spacing allows printing of **superscripts** (characters appearing above the baseline) and **subscripts** (characters appearing below the baseline).
- End-of-paper and end-of-ribbon sensors — a light flashes or a bell rings when ribbon or paper run out.

A daisywheel

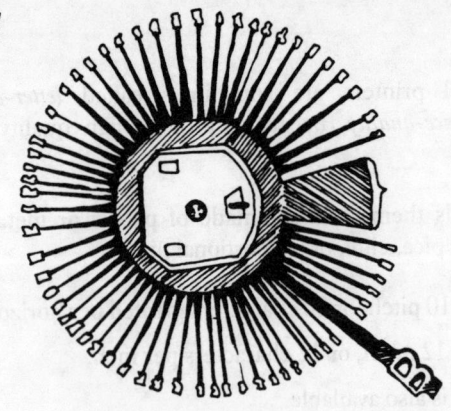

Sample of daisywheel printing

ANSWERS

Listening Test Two A
1. She's a great singer, isn't she?
2. We can do it, can't we?
3. It wasn't cold, was it?
4. We can go with them.
5. They haven't got them, have they?
6. Do you like it, or don't you?

ANSWERS

Listening Test Two A
1. She's a great singer, isn't she?
2. We can do it, can't we?
3. It wasn't cold, was it?
4. We can go with them.
5. They haven't got them, have they?
6. Do you like it, or don't you?

Sample of dot-matrix printing

At least one manufacturer offers a *wide-track* printer. This, as the name implies, is wider than normal printers, and can take larger paper sizes, up to B2 for example. You may also find wide-track printers with two printing heads, which enable you to print with two daisywheels at a time, without changing them.

Daisywheel printers are standard on all word processing systems.

Dot matrix printers

Dot matrix printers are so called because they build a character as a matrix or array of dots using very fine needles. A dot matrix character is the same as that created on a screen.

The printing quality of dot matrix printers is not always as good as that of daisywheels. However, they are improving, and the very good ones are quite acceptable for most work. These are known as **near letter quality (NLQ)** printers.

Some printers have a speed control, allowing you to switch from (slower) NLQ speeds to faster (draft) speeds.

The printing quality of a dot matrix printer is not always as good as that of a daisywheel, but:

- dot matrix printers are a lot faster than daisywheels;
- on dot matrix printers, you can easily alter the characters: their height, their width, their style — you can make them bold, slanted, compact, subscript and superscipt.

Otherwise, dot matrix printers have more or less the same facilities as daisywheels.

Laser printers

Laser printers are very high quality dot matrix printers. Their main features are:

- very high speed printing;
- their use as sheet printers — they can produce 6–8 copies per minute.

Laser printers are often used for short-run printing jobs, eliminating the need for phototypesetting and conventional printing.

Ink-jet printers

Ink-jet printers work by shooting ink on to the paper at high speed.

- They produce very high quality print.
- They are very quiet.

Thermal printers

Thermal printers are rarely used for word processing, as they need special heat-sensitized paper, and are slow.

Paper-handling

Daisywheel printers handle paper using either pressure feed or tractor feed.

Pressure feed is the most common method used, and is identical to that found on a typewriter, in which rubber roller wheels feed the paper around the platen.

Tractor feed is used for a special type of paper, and is an optional accessory on printers.

- The printer has an attachment consisting of two circular belts with protruding studs, one belt at each end of the printer.
- The stationery used has sprocket holes punched on each side of the paper, into which the studs insert, catching and feeding the paper.
- A spring clamp holds the paper against the belt, and gears from the printer motor turn the belts.

A useful but expensive device is the **single-sheet feeder**, which is only available for daisywheel printers. It is basically a tray which holds paper. Under instructions from the printer, it feeds automatically a single sheet into the printer, which saves a lot of time when printing multi-page text.

Dot matrix printers can only feed paper with a tractor feed.

Ribbons

Ribbons for daisywheel printers are usually contained in cartridges, and are called **cartridge ribbons**. Ribbons may be carbon, or fibre.

- **Carbon** — thin plastic film coated with carbon, offering excellent print quality, but rather a short life. They are also expensive.

- **Fibre** — textile, or more common, nylon, treated with ink; not as neat as carbon, but cheaper and longer-lasting.

Carbon ribbons are further classified as single- or multi-strike.

- **Single-strike** — basically, this means that the ribbon can only be used once.

- **Multi-strike** — the ribbon moves only a little bit after each character is struck, and there is enough carbon for several impressions.

Fibre ribbons have a life of around 1 million characters; carbon ribbons are good only for about 300,000 characters.

Dot matrix printer ribbons are contained in spools (as in a typewriter) or in cartridges, and are usually fibre.

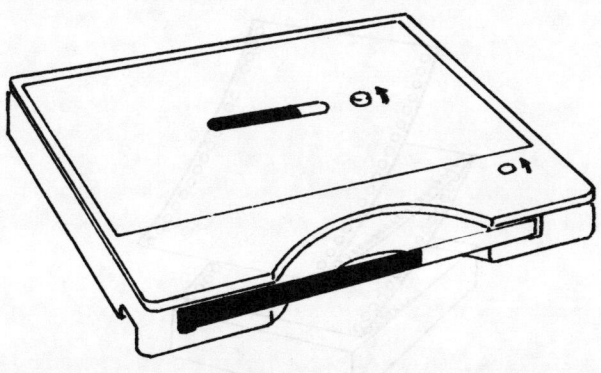

Ribbon (in cartridge)

Stationery

Word processing stationery is of two types: single-sheet or continuous.

The building blocks of a word processor 25

- **Single-sheet** — individual sheets, such as the standard A4, which can be plain, or pre-printed with your company name or other information.

- **Continuous** — sheets held together by perforations at the top and bottom; on the sides, there are sprocket holes, which enable use by a tractor feed.

Single-sheet stationery conforms to the International Paper Size scheme, and the sheets are given a letter/number designation, such as A4, B2, A5, etc. Size is sometimes also expressed in inches or centimetres.

Continuous stationery comes in a variety of sizes, and your tractor feed will determine the maximum size you can use. Since the belts on a tractor are movable, you can use many sizes of paper. Continuous stationery can also be plain or pre-printed.

You also have a wide selection of self-adhesive labels, for jobs like address labels, product labels, and so forth. These come on a continuous backing sheet, to be used with a tractor feed.

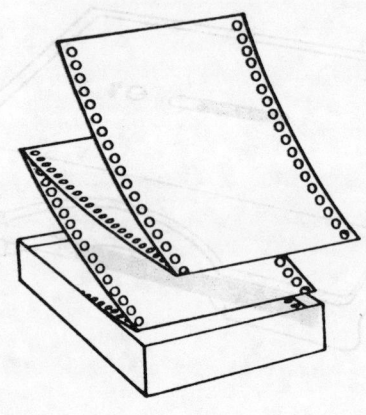

Continuous stationery

Communications

Often, it is necessary for text which has been created and edited on a word processor to be sent to a different location — another word processor in a branch office, for example.

Rather than printing the text on paper and sending it by mail, electronic means can be used, in which text is sent by wires. A communications facility on a word processor enables such electronic means to be used.

- **Communications** (in plural) means the exchange of text or other information between a word processor and some other piece of equipment.

- 'Exchange' means the word processor can both send text to, and receive text from, another device.

Standards

The ways in which text or other information is exchanged between a word processor and other device (in fact, between any electronic devices) are defined by internationally agreed standards. These standards are really protocols.

- **Protocol**, in both human and computer terms, is a set of rules governing the exchange of information.

Protocol comprises rules for speed, timing, the use of interfaces, error detection, and emulation. These are rather technical, but you may still be interested.

Speed

The receiving device must accept text at the same rate that the word processor sends (transmits) it; this is like tuning your radio to the transmitter's frequency. Communications equipment has a range of speeds, which can be set to correspond to the receiving device's capabilities.

Timing

During transmission, the word processor and receiving device must each 'know' what the other is doing, i.e. they must be co-ordinated. This means that they must keep in step with respect to time — this is called *synchronization*. There are two ways to synchronize transmission, and the one used depends on what device you need to communicate with.

Interface

The connection between a word processor and another device is accomplished using an interface. The interface defines:

- the way the sprockets, plugs, and wires are interconnected;
- the number of wires used to carry text;
- the properties (voltage, speed, timing, etc.) the electronic signals have.

Again, the choice of interface depends on the protocol, and the receiving device.

Error detection

Any electronic exchange of information between devices is subject to distortion or other modification during transmission (crossed or 'noisy' telephone lines are familiar examples). To ensure the integrity of the text, error detection is included in communications equipment. As an example,

- certain codes are appended to each character within the text as it is sent;
- when the text is received, these codes are checked to see whether they correspond to the appropriate character — if not, the text will have to be re-transmitted.

There are many ways of detecting errors, which depend on the particular protocol.

Emulation

In the computer industry, certain combinations of speed, timing, interface, and error detection method have been embodied in certain well-known and common pieces of computer hardware — a particular manufacturer's VDU for instance.

- If your word processor has the same speed, timing, interface and error detection as these pieces of hardware, the word processor is said to be **emulating** them.
- In effect, the word processor 'pretends' it is just another computer terminal. The receiving device can't tell the difference.

28 Word Processing

- Specific emulation on the part of the word processor makes it easier for it to be connected to other equipment. For example, if your word processor has 2780/3780/3770 emulation, you can connect it to many types of IBM computer.

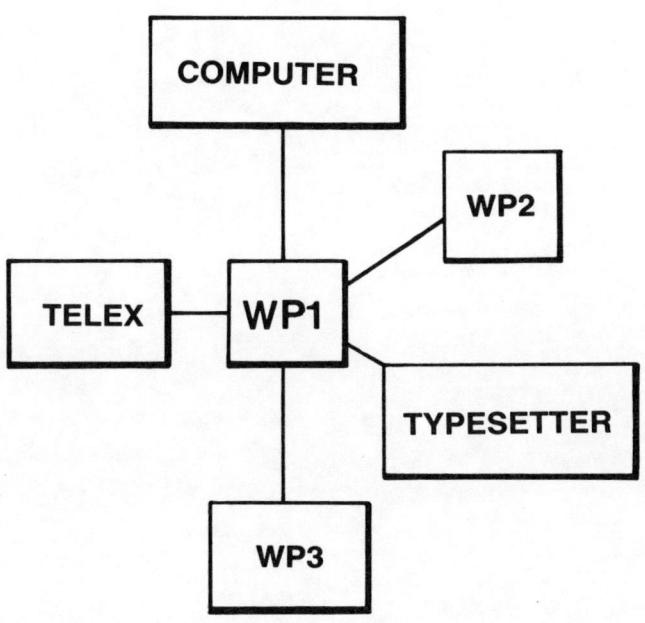

Some of the devices you can link to a WP

Word processing communications equipment comprises hardware, in the form of a small bolt-on unit, and some software.

- The hardware contains all the electronics for the interface, speed and timing control, etc.

- The software allows you to 'fine tune' the hardware for a specific make of equipment.

What can a word processor communicate with? There is a multitude of devices — typesetters, computers, telex machines and other word processors. What about the actual connection?

The building blocks of a word processor 29

- For short distances (within an office), length of wire are used.
- For longer distances (between offices), telephone lines are used.

Remember that communications is a two-way process: the word processor can both transmit and receive text.

3 A session at the word processor

The principal features

The comments in this section are brief and general guidelines to the use of a word processor. Although the principles are the same for all machines, actual procedures will vary a lot among manufacturers. Some features may be more sophisticated than presented here; other features may be included that are not described here. The important thing is to remember the names of these features and what they do.

Text entry

The first activity in word processing is entering text. It is also the easiest to learn and perform, and to which proportionally the largest amount of time is devoted in everyday use.

Switching on

After switching on the word processor, you'll have to insert a special disk, called the *systems disk*, into one of the disk drives.

- The **systems disk** must always be inserted after switching the equipment on.

- The software that makes the word processor work is transferred from the disk to the memory. This transfer takes a few seconds to complete.

- Once the transfer is complete, the systems disk may be removed. In some systems it, or another systems disk, might be needed for some applications, and so remains in the drive.

At this stage, on some systems, you could be asked to key in a date and some other information. Once this information is keyed in, the screen clears, and a *status line* appears, usually at the top of the screen.

- A **status line** shows you the state of the work you are doing. Among other things, it shows you:

- the position of the cursor on the screen, specified as a horizontal line number and position within the line;

- the disk drive being used to store text;

- what activities are being performed by the word processor at a given time;

- line spacing, printing pitch and page length, which will be used to print text at a later stage.

Underneath the status line is a ruler. A **ruler** shows you the current left and right margin, and tab settings.

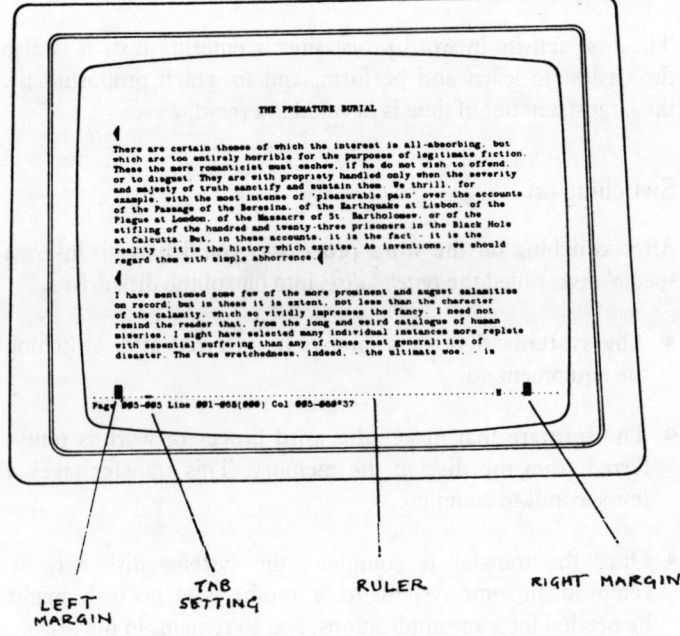

- Left and right **margins** specify the physical boundaries of the text, and are expressed in character positions. For example,

32 Word Processing

a left margin set to 10 and a right margin set to 70 means that each line of text will take up 61 characters.

- **Tab** settings specify the position on the screen to which the cursor will move when the TAB key is pressed. This saves you pressing the space bar.

Left and right margin and tab settings can be changed at any time in the course of entering text. For example, if you are quoting an extract from some other source, each line of the quote would be shorter than the main text. As the settings change, the ruler will show the new values.

When you switch on, the system pre-sets the right and left margins, and sometimes also the tab settings. These are the *default values*.

- A **default value** is one that the system takes on automatically, in the absence of any entries from you.

Of course, the default values can be changed at any time.

Keying text

Once you have defined margins and tabs, you can key text. Keying text is straightforward, as in a typewriter, and usually starts at the top of the screen. This position is often called the HOME position.

- The letters are in lower case; to have capitals, you must press the SHIFT key.

- The SHIFT LOCK is used to keep all the letters as capitals. Additionally, a CAPS LOCK key can be used to key in capitals and numbers, without SHIFTing. Usually, there is a little light to show you if either LOCK key is used.

As text is typed, the status line will show the new position of the cursor.

Simple typing mistakes may be corrected in two ways:
- if the mistake is nearby, the BACKSPACE key may be used. Pressing this key will move the cursor one position to the left, and possibly remove a character. The key is pressed until the mistake is reached, and the correct text is keyed in. Alternatively, some systems will not remove a character, which

means you can only use this to correct mistakes without entering more characters. Of course, you can add or remove characters, and the way to do this will be described later.

- For a mistake that is somewhere else on the screen, the CURSOR CONTROL keys are used, to position the cursor at the mistake. (These are the four or five keys with the arrows on them.) Characters may then be added or removed, or you can type over the wrong ones.

Automatic **centering** is a feature found on all word processors.

- After typing in the text (a heading, for example) pressing a couple of keys will place the text in the middle of the margin settings.

Automatic **underlining** is also present on most word processors, and is turned 'on' or 'off' by a couple of keystrokes.

- Instead of typing text, backspacing and underlining, you need only type the text — the underline appears automatically under each character as it is typed.

The TAB key is often used for indenting paragraphs, or other text, such as the entries in a table of contents.

- To **indent** is to begin a line of text a certain number of spaces away from the left margin. The position at which the text is to start is defined by the tab setting.

Hyphenation

As a line of text is typed, the cursor moves to the right, until it reaches the right margin. Often, a word is too long to be contained on the line.

- If this is the case, **wraparound** occurs. The whole word is removed from the line, and automatically placed at the beginning of the next line.

This is very useful, since it allows you to keep typing without having to constantly check if a word will fit on a line, and without having to mark the end of a line, as with the carriage return in a typewriter.

There is a disadvantage to wraparound — often a word can be *hyphenated*, thereby improving the appearance of the text.

- **Hyphenation** is the division of a word into two parts if it can't fit on one line. The first part of the word is ended with a hyphen (-).

Some systems automatically hyphenate words for you, but none of the methods used is successful. All automatic hyphenation involves using formulae to calculate the position of the hyphen. The results are often disappointing, if not amusing.

Hyphens are of two types: required or discretionary.

- A **required hyphen** is one that occurs naturally in a word — *re-enter* and *co-educational*, for example. Required hyphens are always retained as part of the word.

- A **discretionary hyphen** is one that is inserted in a word to tidy up problems associated with wraparound.

On most systems, discretionary hyphens are inserted between words in the following ways:

- A **hot zone** (or **soft zone**) is specified. A **hot zone** is an area in a line to the left of the right margin, whose width (i.e. number of characters) you can specify.

- A word which starts in the hot zone is detected by the system.

- If the end of a word (i.e. the space after the last character) is within the hot zone, the cursor moves to the next line, and typing continues automatically.

- If the word can't fit in the hot zone, you must make a decision about hyphenation. If a suitable place for a hyphen is found, pressing the hyphen key places the hyphen in the required position. The remainder of the word is carried over to the next line, and the text automatically readjusted.

As you key in text, the screen fills up until there is no more room to display text. When this happens, the text **scrolls**.

- In order to make room on the display for a new line of text, the top line disappears, and a blank line appears at the bottom of the display. Text can now be keyed in that line.

- Text can be scrolled up or down, and sometimes sideways in some systems, using the cursor control keys.

A session at the word processor 35

You've seen that text wraps around automatically as you key it, so you needn't worry about line endings. However, there are times when you need to somehow mark the end of a line.

- To mark the end of an artificially short line (such as a line in an address) or the end of a section of text (a paragraph, etc.), the RETURN key is used. This key may simply be labelled with an arrow (↵).

There is one key which you will always use when issuing the word processor with commands. The commands to the system are the same as any other commands: there is a verb (such as SET) and an object (such as TAB).

- To have the system perform the command, you must end the command with a special key, which is variously called ACCEPT, EXECUTE, ENTER, DO , GO. Sometimes, the RETURN key is used.

- Most commands need to be concluded with such a key. This is useful — you can make sure your command is right before proceeding with it.

Pieces of text are called different things by different system manufacturers.

- Most complete units of text (a report, or letter, for example) tend to be called **documents**. The term **file** is used sometimes.

- Documents are usually subdivided into pages. A **page** can be of any length — a screen page of 20 lines, or a paper page of 60 lines are two examples. The length of a page can be set and changed at any time, depending on what form it takes (screen or paper), and on how large a unit of text the system can accommodate.

Storage

One of the two most important features of a word processor is its means for storing text for future use.

Saving text
- To put a document on a disk is to **save** it; you may find other words similar in meaning being used, such as *memorize* or *store*.

To save a document, you must first identify it. This means giving it a name or other reference under which it will be filed. There are as many ways to identify documents as there are word processors — no two systems are alike.

Many systems force you to identify the document before keying it. You must give it a name.

- The document name can usually be any combination of letters, numbers and other symbols; the length of the name depends on the system, but typical values are between 8 and 20 characters.

Other systems automatically assign a number to the document — you have no choice in the name, and must refer to the document by its number.

Whether using name or number identifiers, most systems let you add a description to the document; this is usually just one short line in which the contents of the document are described.

The size of the unit of text that can be filed also varies considerably among systems.

- Some systems force you to work with many small units, sometimes as small as a screenful. Each unit will have the same document name, but may be suffixed by a number.

- Some systems will automatically save the document as the buffer is filled up. With others, you have to save it manually.

A disk has a finite capacity for storing text, and if you try to save a document which will not fit into the available disk space, you will get a message saying DISK FULL, or something similar.

The index

The **index** gives you useful information about the documents stored on the disk. The index is displayed on the screen when the appropriate command is typed. The index shows you:

- the name of the document, or other reference under which it is stored;

- the size of the document — how much room it takes up on the disk, measured in characters, pages, or other units;

- the space remaining for storage.

A session at the word processor

The document index of a disk

```
DOCUMENT INDEX

DRIVE 0      264        (037)
INVOICES 1              LETTERS 2
INVOICES 2              PRICES
STATEMENTS              DISCOUNTS
LETTERS 1

DRIVE 1      379        (021)
PURCHASES               SALES
DELIVERIES              A/C NOS
REFUNDS                 INSURANCE
CREDITS
```

This is the minimum amount of information you'll see. Often, there is much more given, such as:

- the date on which the document was created;
- a description of the document (if you keyed one in when identifying the document).

You could find still more information — the date of revision (when you last edited the document), or the number of times the document has been printed.

The index can be printed on paper. This will help you identify the disks, since you can attach the index to the disk's wallet.

In order to work on a document that has been saved, you have to transfer it from the disk to the buffer. This is to **recall** it. On some systems, recall is very simple: all you do is position the cursor to the document's name, and press the appropriate key.

'Editing' the disk

As you use your word processor, you will have accumulated documents that you no longer need. You should get rid of them. This is sometimes called *housekeeping*.

- 'Getting rid' of a document from a disk is called **deleting**; just as you delete words from a line, you delete documents from a disk.

- All word processors have a command to delete documents.

When you delete a document, all its details (name, size, etc.) are removed from the index. But,

- the document is not actually erased from the disk; rather, the area where it was stored is marked as 'free'.

Next time you come to store a document, the system will try to find a free area. If it does, your document is stored there. That the document is not actually erased is, in most cases, of no consequence to you. There is an exception, however.

What happens if you delete a document, realizing later that you deleted the wrong one? If you haven't got a copy, it could be unfortunate. For this reason, some manufacturers include a **document recovery** procedure. This is how it works:

- You enter the identity of the document to be recovered. The system will try to find it (remember — the document hasn't been erased)

- If the document is found, the area on the disk where it's stored is marked as 'occupied', and the document's name and other details are put in the index.

Document recovery is usually successful. It is not foolproof though, and fails in some cases. It's almost certain to fail in the following case:

- if your disk is nearly full, and you've deleted a document, storing another one in its place.

- Since there is little room left on the disk, the system found the last free area (which was previously holding your deleted document) and stored the new document there.

- If you try to recover, the system will not find the document, since it has been over-recorded by the new document.

Document recovery procedures should not be abused. As it happens, there is a convenient way to create a duplicate of every document.

What other 'editing' can you do to a disk? Consider a case in which a document was stored under one name, but you've decided to call it something else.

- All word processors let you change the name of a document. This is called **renaming** the document.

If you need to rename a document, you'll be asked for its current name, and its new name. The system will rename the document, and put the new name in the index. (Nothing else has changed — only the new name is put in the index.)

Incidentally, when the word processor asks you questions (such as current and new document name in renaming), it issues a prompt.

- A **prompt** is a cue (a question) to give the word processor some specific information. (*Prompt* is also a verb, e.g. the system *prompts* you for information.)

Duplication

You should ALWAYS make duplicates of your documents. Floppy disks wear out, get coffee spilled on them, and get subjected to other forms of mutilation. If one of your disks gets mutilated, and you haven't got a duplicate, you'll have to re-enter all the text on it.

- All word processors have a procedure to duplicate disks.
- You can duplicate an individual document, or the whole contents of the disk.
- You should get into the habit of making duplicates — after first entering the text, and after any editing.

The duplication procedures (performed automatically by the system under your instruction) entails 'reading' a document from one disk, and 'writing' it on to another disk, in the second disk drive. The procedure takes at most a couple of minutes.

Formatting

There is one other procedure you may come across, although this depends on your machine. This is **formatting**, and must be done before you use the disk.

- When you buy a disk, it has nothing on it — it is literally a piece of plastic.

- The system needs to 'know' where documents are to be stored, so the disk is organized into a series of areas that are to hold text. This is rather like putting a map on the disk's surface.

- Formatting consists of defining these areas. They may be called *sectors*, *segments*, or something else.

Formatting, if required, also takes around a couple of minutes to complete. With some systems, the disks are purchased from the manufacturer, and they are formatted before being sent to you. Hence, you don't have to do it yourself.

Remember, though, that whether you or the manufacturer does it, disks must be formatted before they are used.

Switching off

You should switch off only after all your text is saved on disk. Follow the manufacturer's recommendations for switching the system off, but in any case make sure the following are done:

- any unwanted documents are deleted;
- any 'housekeeping' tasks, such as renaming documents, are done;
- the disks are removed from the machine and stored safely.

Of course, you may want to print and edit the text before you switch off.

Printing

Once text has been entered and saved, it is usually printed, so the author can proofread it and make any corrections.

Concurrency

New and more sophisticated word processors have been designed to process two jobs concurrently. For example, while one document is being printed, you are free to key or edit another, different document, without having to wait for the printing to finish. Without this concurrency, you would have to wait until the printing finished before doing anything else.

To accommodate two jobs, the word processor is in effect split into two areas: foreground and background.

- **Foreground** handles all the jobs associated with the entry and display of text — all jobs that need your attention.

- **Background** handles those jobs which can be done without any intervention from you — printing text is one example, although some automatic editing functions can also be done in background.

The status line will show you what is in background. Remember, background and foreground are two totally separate and independent areas: you always work in foreground, and the system takes care of background.

With printing, some manufacturers take concurrency one step further: they give you a print queue or spooler.

- A **print queue** is like any other queue: things (in this case documents) are lined up, awaiting some action.

Consider an example: a number of separate documents have to be printed one after the other.

- Even if printing is done in background, you still have to interrupt your foreground work, to put the next document into background and print it.

- Using a print queue, you specify what documents are to be printed, and in what order. The system takes the first document in the queue, prints it, takes the next document off the queue, and so on; all this is done in background, automatically, without disturbing your foreground work.

- In effect, three jobs are now done by the system at the same time.

There is a certain maximum number of documents that you can have in the queue.

Spool is an acronym of **s**imultaneous **p**eripheral **o**peration **o**n-**l**ine, which, in computer terms, describes the operation of a print queue. *Spool* and *print queue* are two names for the same thing.

Pagination

Since the document is printed on a fixed length of paper, you must specify how many lines of text are to appear on each page. This is called **pagination**. The length of a page appears in the status line. You also have to specify the line spacing (i.e. single, double or 1½ spacing. Other spacings may also be possible).

- When the system paginates a document, it scans it from the beginning, and inserts page breaks after the specified number of lines.

- A **page break** is simply a code to the printer instructing it to eject the paper, feed a new sheet in and resume printing.

There are a few things to remember about pagination:

- Page breaks are inserted into the text by the system. You (or the system) can override them anytime.

- Overriding page breaks may be necessary; for example, when you need an artificially short page, to accommodate a drawing.

- Page breaks that are inserted by you, overriding the system's, are variously called *forced, hard* or *required* page breaks.

- In text consisting of paragraphs, in which each paragraph is separated by a number of blank lines, you will occasionally find that a page break occurs after the first line of a new paragraph, or before the last line of a paragraph. These lines are called *widow* and *orphan* lines.

- A **widow line** is the first line of a new paragraph that appears at the bottom of the page, by itself. An **orphan line** is the last line of a paragraph, that appears at the top of the page.

- Widow and orphan lines spoil the appearance of printed text, so every system has ways of finding these lines, and readjusting the page line lengths a little to get rid of them.

Most systems let you have headings and footings appear automatically on each page.

- A **heading**, or **header**, is a short piece of text that appears at the top of a page, on every page. The title of a report is one example.

- A **footing**, or **footer**, is like a heading, except it appears at the bottom of the page

Beware: a footing is not the same as a footnote, although these two words are used loosely and interchangeably.

- A **footnote** is a short piece of text that appears at the bottom of a page, giving extra information about material contained within the text. A footnote is always referenced by a number, and belongs only to the page in which it is referenced; i.e. it does not appear on every page.

All systems number pages automatically for you. All you do is specify the starting value. Page numbers can appear at the top or bottom of a page, and are usually Arabic numbers; occasionally, you may find systems that print Roman numbers as well.

Justification

After paginating the text, you have to specify the pitch at which the text is to be printed. Pitch is the number of characters that are printed in one horizontal inch. You can choose from 10 pitch (*pica*), 12 pitch (*elite*), or 15 pitch.

Also, you have to decide whether the text is to be justified.

- Text that has been **justified** has each line 'stretched out', so that the last character appears at the right margin. This gives the text the form of a column.

- **Unjustified** text has each line in its normal length — no 'stretching' is done, and the right-hand side is ragged, which is why it is called **ragged right**. (Sometimes, the printing term *ranged left* is used, meaning that the text is all pressed up against the left margin.)

Text is justified by the system, by inserting a number of tiny spaces between letters in a word, and between words themselves. The actual size of the space is some multiple of a tiny fraction of an inch (between $1/120''$ and $1/60''$).

Too much white space between words and letters also spoils the appearance of text, so you must balance justification with hyphenation, where possible.

You can also print text in proportional pitch, on systems that have this facility. Remember that proportional spacing means

Justified text

```
After    performing    frequently    with
his  family,  it  was  only  in  the  last
decade       that       Jeremy       Menuhin
decided      on     a    career    as    a solo
pianist.     He       includes       in his
programme      works      by      Debussy
and Schubert.
```

```
After   performing   frequently   with
his family, it was only in the last
decade that **Jeremy Menuhin**
decided on a career as a solo
pianist. He includes in his
programme works by **Debussy**
and **Schubert.**
```

Unjustified text (ragged right) with various words in **bold**

each character takes up only the space it needs (*i* needs less space than *m*). Proportionally justified text has a very high-quality appearance. This book was printed with proportional justification (although not on a daisywheel printer).

- Justification can be done in background, as text is being printed, or in foreground, before printing. In the latter case, you can see the results of justification, and make changes if necessary.

- Some systems can display text on the screen in various pitches, and even with pseudo-proportional spacing.

Finally, the text is printed. Here are a couple of other features of printing which most systems have to offer.

- You can insert special codes in your text which, when recognized by the printer, stop the printing. You can change daisywheels, for example, to print some parts of the text in a different font. There will be a key to press to resume printing.

A session at the word processor 45

- You can print text in **bold,** or **emboldened** (as here). Emboldened text is darker, and stands out against normally printed text. Text can be emboldened with overstrike or offset-overstrike, depending on your system.

- **Overstrike** — the same character is repeatedly printed in the same spot.

- **Offset-overstrike** — the character is printed with overstrike, but the daisywheel moves a tiny fraction to the right, and the character printed with overstrike again; as well as being darker, the character is slightly wider, and stands out even more.

- In both cases, the text to be emboldened is marked with special codes. The number of times a character is repeated varies, but often, it is just twice.

Editing

The ease with which text can be edited is the second important distinguishing feature of a word processor. Text can be edited at any time — while it is being keyed, or after keying is complete. Of course, a document can be recalled from the disk and edited. Editing facilities are comprehensive on all word processors.

Deletion

To **delete** means to remove a specified portion of text from a document. Once the text has been deleted, you can't get it back, unless you have the document on disk.

Text can be deleted in two ways, depending on your system.

- The portion of text to be deleted is marked with a special key: the cursor is moved to the beginning of the portion, the key marks it, then the cursor is moved to the end of the portion, and this is again marked. Pressing the DELETE key deletes the portion.

- Each component of text (character, word, line, paragraph or the whole document) has its corresponding key. To delete (say) a word, you press the DELETE and WORD keys, after positioning the cursor to the required word.

Two things are common to both methods:

- the portion of text to be deleted is **highlighted,** which means it is outlined with a bar of light. This gives you a chance to check what you're about to delete.

- As the text is deleted, the rest of the text moves in, taking the place of the deleted text. Word wraparound occurs automatically.

Insertion

To **insert** means to add some text to a document.

You can insert characters by moving the cursor to the required place. You then either press the INSERT and CHARACTER keys (which 'open up' the text) and key in the new characters, or just press INSERT and key as if you're entering text. In both cases the rest of the text adjusts automatically, and again, words wrap around.

- Similarly you can INSERT blank LINEs within text.

Blocks

Often, you need to delete, or move around, sections of text. These sections could be of any length — from a couple of words to several paragraphs. Using the block facilities, you can perform many elaborate cut-and-paste operations.

- A **block** is a portion of text whose length you specify by placing block markers at the beginning and end. A **block marker** is simply a special character or key used to mark the start and end of a block.

- **Cut-and-paste** means marking a block, removing it from one location (*cut*) and inserting it into another location (*paste*).

Word processors have facilities to mark, move, copy, save, delete and recall blocks.

- To **move** a block, you first mark it with the block markers, then position the cursor to where the block is to go. Pressing the MOVE key deletes the block from its original position, and inserts it into the new position. The rest of the text moves to accommodate the block.

- To **copy** a block is the same as to *move* it, except it is not deleted from its original position. Hence, you can duplicate a portion of text without re-keying it.

Saving and recalling blocks can save you a lot of time. Consider the trivial case of typing a few letters, in which the introductory and closing paragraphs are the same, for all the letters. Here's what you might do.

- You would key the introductory paragraph, and save it on disk as a block; likewise for the closing paragraph.

- When you key the letter, instead of keying the introductory paragraph, you recall it from disk, and it is inserted into the letter.

- You then key the rest of the letter, and at the end, you recall the closing paragraph.

Blocks are saved and recalled in the same way as any other document.

Of course, blocks can be deleted from text. The advantage here is that it is easier to mark and delete a block than to use combinations of word, character and line deletions.

Some systems let you temporarily store a block to be copied, either in the buffer or on the disk. This storage is sometimes called a **copy**, or **text register**. It is particularly useful if you have to duplicate a block several times within a document.

Document assembly

A more sophisticated application of blocks is in creating standard paragraphs, or boilerplates.

- A **standard paragraph**, as the name implies, is a paragraph that occurs frequently in different types of documents. **Boilerplate** is the American equivalent.

Consider contracts, which consist of clauses.

- A complete collection of clauses can be keyed, once, and saved on disk. Each clause has its own name or other reference.

- When a contract needs to be drawn up, all you do is state what clauses are needed.

- The word processor will recall each clause, in the order specified, and assemble a complete contract in seconds.

- Once the contract is assembled, you can make any minor changes that may be needed, and print it.

A collection of standard paragraphs on disk is sometimes called a **glossary**.

Assembling documents can be even easier:

- instead of keying the paragraph names manually, you can create a document which has only these names as text.

The system now 'reads' the document, rather than asking you for the names, and assembles the document. The document assembly could even take place in background.

You can also assemble documents by merging separate documents into one. **Merge** really means to append one document to the end of another. You could collate a report by merging the separate sections, for example.

A neat extension of the glossary is the **abbreviation library**. Here's how you could use it:

- You create a set of lines, each line being the full form of an abbreviation; for instance, *magneto-hydrodynamics* could be abbreviated to *mhd*.

- As you key your text, instead of keying the full word, you only key its abbreviation.

- The system automatically substitutes the abbreviation with the full form.

Word processing libraries (also called **dictionaries**) are the same as any other. Of course, glossaries and libraries can be added to, or can have parts deleted. To the system, they're just pieces of text. All you have to do is identify them according to the system's conventions.

Search and replace

If your system hasn't got an abbreviation library facility, you can use the search and replace one, which every system has.

- **Search and replace** means the system searches for a given word, and replaces it with another word, for every time it finds it.

- Typically, the system prompts you with SEARCH FOR WHAT?, to which you answer with the required word; you are then prompted with REPLACE WITH?, and you key the replacement.

- Finally, you must state how many times the replacement is to be done. The system finds the first occurrence, and shows it to you with highlighting.

- If it's correct, you press the appropriate key, and the word is replaced. Likewise for every occurrence of the word.

Search and replace is not confined to only words. This is why the term *string* is used.

- A **string** is a sequence of contiguous characters; 'tex' is a string, as is 'a computer'. Strings can also be special characters, like codes for emboldening.

One of the problems with search and replace is string matching. If you want to find and replace 'AUTHOR', you must key it in capitals, because if you don't, it won't be found. On some systems, searching is more flexible — in the above example, if you keyed the word in lower case, or in a combination of cases, it would still be found.

Another problem is with hyphenated words. If you are searching for a hyphenated string, chances are it won't be found.

Direction of search is yet another constraint. Usually, searching is carried out from the current cursor position to the end of the text — i.e. 'forwards'. If the string is nearer the beginning of the text (before the cursor), it will not be found. Some systems can search 'forwards' and 'backwards'.

One final point: there is a limit to the size of the string that can be searched, which varies from system to system.

To compensate for these problems, search and replace can be done automatically in background, providing you're sure of the string and how many times it occurs.

Reformatting

In the course of editing, you may have inserted new text and deleted unwanted text. The length of the document has probably changed. Before printing the document, you'll have to put in new page breaks.

- To **repaginate** is to insert new page breaks into edited text. It is exactly the same procedure as pagination.

You may have also changed the appearance and layout (**format**) of the text, by changing the margins for example.

- Since changing margins may affect the length of a line and hence any hyphens in it, you'll have to **rehyphenate** the document.

- Any discretionary hyphens will have been dropped, so you again need to tidy up any wraparound problems. Required hyphens, of course, are not dropped.

- Don't forget that justification affects the extent of hyphenation in the document. You may have to unjustify the document, change the margins, hyphenate, and then rejustify.

A few extras

Some systems give you extra tools with which you can create and edit text. Here are a few you may come across.

Spelling dictionary

At first, a spelling dictionary, to automatically check and correct the spelling of every word in the document, seems attractive. However, there seems to be more against it than for it.

- A spelling dictionary must be accurate. This sounds trivial, but no dictionary is yet perfect.

- The methods used to check words are rather complicated. Most times, the correct word is found, but words with incorrect prefixes or suffixes are sometimes passed. Occasionally, totally different words are substituted!

- Spelling correction facilities are only as good as the size of the dictionary. On a floppy disk system, storage for a comprehensive dictionary is limited.

- Spelling correction must be fast. Again, on a floppy system, searching through a long document can take a long time.

- If you use an extensive technical vocabulary, you'll have to create a separate dictionary yourself.

Careful proofreading is usually a less frustrating alternative.

One handy use of a spelling dictionary is for checking the spelling of foreign words.

At least one manufacturer offers foreign-language dictionaries that allow you to check the spelling of up to 150,000 words, in Norwegian, Swedish, Danish, Dutch, Spanish, Italian, French and German.

Foreign languages, symbols and line graphics

Foreign languages

Some systems give you facilities for creating text in foreign languages. Romance and Germanic languages (those having the Latin alphabet) are the easiest to work with, since in most cases, you only need to enter accents.

- These accents, which usually appear above a certain letter, include ´, `, ^, ~, ¨, ", °, ˘.

- Sometimes, accents appear below a letter, as with the French ç and Rumanian ț.

- Occasionally, different or modified letters are used: β in German, or ø and æ in some Scandinavian languages.

On some systems, optional foreign-language keyboards are available. With others, you'll have to use a combination of keys to create the accents. Sometimes, accented letters are part of the system's character set, such as é, è, à, ö, ü.

Obviously, the daisywheel must have the right accents. Many foreign language daisywheels have the necessary letters already accented.

- The best way to check what is on the daisywheel is to create a document, in which each line is a combination of keystrokes of one keyboard row. When you print it, you can see which characters correspond to which keystrokes.

Some things to remember:

- Hyphenation and wraparound could be troublesome procedures in some languages, because of different (longer) word lengths.

- Dutch and German are notorious, because of their long compounded words.

- Some languages, such as Russian, have only a few Latin letters. Also, the size of the alphabet could be different (Russian, for example, has 32 letters in its alphabet).

- Some languages, such as Arabic and Hebrew, are read and written from right to left. This can create considerable problems. Also, they have a completely different character set.

- The availability of a foreign-language spelling dictionary could be important in your choice of system

Symbols

All physical sciences and most social sciences use special symbols to express things. A symbol in this case is simply a special character representing an idea or procedure. If you process a lot of scientific text, you will need means to create these symbols.

- Many symbols are taken from the Greek alphabet, such as μ, π, Ω. Others are artificial, such as ∞ and $\triangle$.

Superscripts and subscripts are extensively used. For example:

- $y = \frac{c}{2}(e^{\frac{x}{c}} + e^{-\frac{x}{c}})$

- $Fe(CN)_6^{3-} + e^- = Fe(CN)_6^{4-}$

Superscripts and subscripts are easy to create and print on all systems. The printed appearance won't be so neat, though; subscripts and superscripts are printed in the same size as other characters.

Most systems will only let you create the standard mathematical symbols and the letters in the Greek alphabet. For out-of-the-ordinary symbols, such as those found in astrology and astronomy, you'll have to see first if there is a daisywheel available. Then you have to find on the keyboard the keys that print the symbols you want.

Line graphics

If you want to put boxes around text, or rule off columns, you will need a line graphics facility.

- With this facility, lines are easy to draw on the screen and print on paper; you are restricted to vertical and horizontal lines, though.

- The appearance of the lines on paper will be rather poor. A daisywheel prints continuous lines as a series of __ (underlines).

- The lines will have kinks in them, and corners will not be perfect.

Calculator

A word processor with an in-built calculator lets you do simple arithmetic on sets of figures, and gives you an extra check on the accuracy of totals, etc.

- You will get at least three basic arithmetic operations: addition, subtraction and multiplication. Division may not be included in some systems. In others, it may not work very well, giving you limited accuracy.

- Usually, there will be a way to calculate percentages and column totals.

- Occasionally, you may find facilities to calculate averages, or automatically print totals in bold.

Traditionally, the main problem with working with figures has been lining up the decimal points. The word processor solves this problem by giving you a DECIMAL TAB key.

- You set your tab at the position of the decimal point.

- To enter a figure, you press DECIMAL TAB, and key the numbers. They are filled in from right to left. Numbers after the decimal point are filled in normally, after pressing the . key.

A *numeric keypad* (a separate numeric area on the keyboard) is helpful if you have to key a lot of numbers.

A numeric keypad

List processing

One of the most popular applications of list processing is the creation and printing of 'personalized' letters, for direct mailings, reminder notices, and circular letters.

There are two parts to list processing:

- creating a standard letter, with spaces left for text that changes from letter to letter, such as name and address, salutation, etc.;

- creating a list of names, addresses, salutations and other *variables* that change from letter to letter.

When you create the standard letter (or other document), you will have to mark the places where the variables are to go.

- These marks are variously called **stop codes, start codes** or **switch codes**.

- These codes appear in the same order as the variables in the list, and there must be as many codes as there are variables.

Say you needed to send a letter to 100 people, telling them about a forthcoming event. Here's what you would do.

- Create the 'standard' part of the letter (the details of the event).

- At the top of the letter, put in the stop codes where the name and address are to go, one code for each line.

- Save the letter, and create a list of the people, each detail on a separate line. You also save the list.

The system does the rest. It:

- takes the first line from the variables list, and puts it in the place of the first stop code of the letter.

This substitution is carried out until there are no more stop codes in the letter, whence it is printed. Then the first stop code of the letter is substituted with the next variable line, and the above process repeated until the list of variables is exhausted.

This is another job that could be (and usually is) done in background.

Of course, the variable list can be edited like any other document, and since it's on disk, you won't have to key it again if you need to send another letter to the same people.

Records management

Records management is a facility for creating, storing, and selectively printing information. It is a comprehensive facility on the systems that have it.

Records management comprises four activities:

- creating records;
- editing records;
- selecting and sorting records;
- printing records.

To understand what a record is, you must know about files.

- A **file** is a set of related records.

Files are notional entities, conceptually the same as any other. In a *correspondence file*, for example, the records are letters. All a file does is impose a structure on information. For example,

- a file may consist of all your current clients, or all the products you manufacture;
- each record within the file contains details of the client or product — name, phone number, price, quantity on hand.
- each subdivision (detail) within the record is called a **field**.

So, *fields* make up *records*, and records make up a *file*.

Consider now the four activities within records management.

Creating records

This is the first step. You have to define the record as follows:

- number of fields — how many fields each record is to have;
- type of field — **alphanumeric** (letters and numbers) or **numeric** (numbers only);
- length of field — how many characters each field will hold.

Each record will have the same type and length of field, and the same number of fields. Once you've defined the record, you can put in all the details, and save the file on disk.

Editing records

You can insert, delete or change any detail in the record, within your record definition; i.e. you can't add more fields to the record without re-entering all the information, from scratch.

Selecting and sorting records

Selection and sorting are the really impressive features of records management. For example, you can select from your file of 'clients' all those who live in a given town; in your 'product' file, you can select all the products with a particular product code.

You may also want to sort these selected records.

- To **sort** means to arrange or order information into a predetermined sequence.

You could sort all your clients in a particular town into alphabetical order, by surname.

There's a lot more you can do. You can impose some conditions on the selection; for example,

- select all clients in a particular town who owe you over a certain amount of money;
- select all products with a given product code that have been sold after a given date.

Again, you could sort these records into any order, by increasing amounts, for example.

There are usually eight conditions that you can specify. You can select records with a field

- equal to some predetermined value (=)
- less than some predetermined value (<)
- greater than some predetermined value (>)
- greater than or equal to some value (>=)
- less than or equal to some value (<=)
- not equal to some value (≠)

You can combine any of these conditions with the words <u>AND</u> and <u>OR</u>.

Looking at the 'outstanding amounts' examples again, you would express the selection as follows:

- select all clients with TOWN = ... <u>AND</u> AMOUNT OWING > ....

On some systems, you can do calculations on fields. In the 'clients' file again, you could keep a running total of outstanding amounts.

58 Word Processing

Printing records

Once you've selected and sorted your records, you'll want to print them.

- In some systems, records are printed as they are selected.
- In others, another file is created, which is then printed.

You can sometimes combine records management and list processing.

- Instead of printing the records, pertinent details could be saved as a list of variables, which can then be combined with a standard letter — to produce a reminder notice, for instance.

Records management is a worthwhile extra, which gives your word processor some of the facilities of a computer.

User programming

This is a misleading term, since it can have two different meanings.

- In its widest usage, user programming means that you can assign one key to represent many individual keystrokes.

In a word processor that has communications, you may often need to send a document to another workstation; normally, this procedure would need many keystrokes.

- With user programming, you assign one key to contain these keystrokes.
- This key is sometimes called a *user-defined key*.
- Now, with only one keystroke, you can make those many keystrokes occur automatically, thereby reducing time and likelihood of mistakes.

Usually, any combination of keystrokes can be assigned one key. Of course, you can change the assignment at any time.

Instead of having user-defined keys, some systems make you create a document containing the keystrokes. The end result is the same, since the system now reads the document.

In its other sense, user programming means that you can use your word processor to write computer programs, and hence use it as a computer.

- You could use the word processor for non-WP tasks, such as invoicing.
- You could create facilities to handle text in a way that the word processor can't.

Consider the second case: if, for example, you created a teaching text, and needed every word in it to be put in a list and sorted alphabetically; a program could be written to do so, extending the scope of the word processor.

Using a word processor as a computer is not as easy as it sounds.

- Word processors are sold as word processors, not general-purpose computers.
- There is very little, if any, commercial software — such as invoicing or financial modelling — available.
- Most times, you would have to write the software yourself, or get it written for you.
- Unless you are an experienced programmer, writing your own software could pose problems.
- Usually, very little, if any, supporting material (such as guides to programming, etc.) is given. You are 'left to your own devices'.

With the popularity of small, personal computers and the widespread use of easy-to-learn programming languages, you might think that learning to program is not a problem. Bear these points in mind, though:

- As with natural languages, certain styles and techniques are used when writing software in computer languages.
- In theory, as long as a program does its job, it doesn't matter how it does it.
- In practice, this is not so: software is written to do the job at maximum speed, conserving resources (such as memory and disk space), and to give you maximum benefit and ease of use.

Software written in such a way is elegant — it is efficient. To write efficient software, you need a knowledge of:

- the computer's (or word processor's) design details;
- the application (e.g. financial model) being programmed;
- certain generally accepted procedures for performing a given task, and certain procedures specific to your task.

These procedures are called **algorithms** — they state the rules necessary to perform the task efficiently.

The art and science of writing software is called **programming**. Whether programming is easy or not is a contentious issue:

- Programming is easy, since computer languages are easy to learn and use.
- Programming is not easy, since to write efficient software requires more than just a knowledge of a computer language.

Computer programmers are classed as professionals, and must have training and experience. For personal computing, such discipline is not required.

For more sophisticated work, a knowledge of algorithms is important.

However, remember that there are many computer professionals around. If you do have a particular job that must be done on a word processor, chances are you could get software written for you. Sometimes, an existing program could be converted to work on your machine.

Unless you're experienced in computers, remember that outside help may be needed.

Integration

If you are using word processing software, you may be able to incorporate material from another program into word-processed text. Examples are:

- figures, tables etc. from spreadsheet calculations;
- graphs from a spreadsheet program;
- pie charts, diagrams, etc. from a graphics program;
- lists, summaries etc. from a database.

Or you may be using a word processing package which is one of several programs supplied all on one disk and designed to work together in this way. Software of this kind is called **integrated software**.

A typical integrated software package might consist of five programs:

- word processing;
- a database;
- a spreadsheet;
- a graphics facility;
- telecommunications.

To simplify these terms:

- a database is a type of filing system;
- spreadsheets are sophisticated calculation programs;
- graphics programs present information visually;
- the telecommunications element allows the user to link up with outside information sources such as Prestel, or to communicate with other computers. (This usually happens via a telephone line.)

The difference between incorporating data from another program into word-processed text and using fully integrated software is that:

- with separate programs, you have to read (i.e. transfer) information from one disk to another, which is time-consuming;
- integrated software contains all the programs on one disk. Data can therefore be incorporated into your text easily, without loading a new program.

Mouse

A **mouse** is a small device which you hold in your hand and move around your desk top. As it moves, so does a **pointer** or cursor on the screen. Moving around the screen with a mouse is simpler than using the keyboard arrows.

The mouse is particularly useful if your word processing software uses **icons**. These represent graphically on the screen various functions or operations of the program.

For example, a waste-paper basket may represent the command 'dump' or 'delete', a clipboard may represent 'notes', a folder the command 'file'. Point at the icon using the mouse, and the computer carries out the command.

Some computers allow you to touch the screen instead of using a mouse.

Windows

With some programs — particularly in integrated software — you can split the screen into several parts. Each **window** holds a different file, or a different part of the same file. You can copy or move data very easily between windows, especially with a mouse controller.

Some word processing programs allow you to create up to eight windows. However, if you have more than three or four files open at once, you'll end up with a very cluttered screen.

The process of creating these windows on screen is called **windowing**.

4 Questions and answers

Analyzing the needs

It is very easy to justify the purchase of a word processing system if you produce a lot of text. Although deciding on word processing is easier than deciding on computerization, a word processor is not just an expensive typewriter.

Getting a word processing system still means spending a lot of money, so the right questions must be asked and properly answered before committing yourself.

Here is a guide to your approach to word processing.

- Determine what work needs to be done on word processors. Check with all sources of text.

- Check if there are any special requirements the word processor must meet.

- Keep a set of figures: types and sizes of documents, number of pages, frequency of revision or change, number of copies made, and so on. Write everything down.

- Check how often similar documents occur, and at what intervals.

- Become familiar with the concepts and jargon of word processing.

- Read related periodicals. There are still very few books on word processing available.

- Select a few system suppliers, and arrange demonstrations.

- In the light of your first exposure to word processors, repeat the first two steps above, and see more suppliers.

- If you need to, get help or advice from other people in your position, or those who already use word processors.

- Some suppliers and some word processing bureaux offer a consultancy service. You may want to use this service if the cost isn't prohibitive.

If you decide that a word processing system can help you, there are still a few questions to be answered.

- How many word processors do you need? If you need more than one, will text have to be shared among several workstations?

- Will you need extensive computer as well as word processing facilities?

- Word processing systems do some things very well, other thinks not so well. What are your applications that are critical in performance?

Remember that you may have to recruit or train operators, or train people who originate text.

Consider the costs of word processing. You'll find that:

- in some areas, the time saved by using word processing machines over conventional ones results in a lot of money being saved;

- in other areas, there may not be any financial advantage in using word processors. Cost, if you can, your current text production.

You'll also find that there are:

- one-off costs, such as the hardware and training, desks and chairs and installation costs (if any);

- on-going costs, such as disks, ribbons, maintenance contracts. (Maintenance contracts are very expensive, but not always very useful. Some insurance companies offer 'breakdown' policies which can solve part of the problem.)

Finally,

- Word processing technology is changing rapidly. You might consider waiting for technology to improve or prices to drop.

- You have to start somewhere.

- Make the right choice in the first place, and you'll have a system that will help you for a long time.

- DON'T RUSH IN!

Recognizing the solutions

Choices

You have two choices of word processing equipment: dedicated and computer-based. What follows is a description, together with a few advantages and disadvantages of each.

Dedicated systems

A dedicated word processor is one designed for word processing *and nothing else*. Unless you already have a computer, or are thinking of getting one, a dedicated system is probably better than a computer-based one.

The greatest advantage of a dedicated system is that it is designed and built with only word processing in mind.

- All the machine's internal and external features are designed and built with only word processing in mind.

- The keyboard only has the keys that are needed. Each major task has its own key, with a unique label. Often, keys have colour or symbol labels, for easier use.

- Keyboards are always detached from the screen, so they can be positioned according to individual preferences.

- The screen and display are often better than those on a computer. Tilting and swivelling screens are one example.

- Hardware design takes word processing into account, in terms of available memory, communications, options, size, type and number of characters on the screen, to name a few examples.

- The software takes full advantage of the hardware. It is very fast, and of good quality, because it was designed for use by non-computer people.

What all these features mean is that a dedicated system is easier to use than a computer-based system.

That the word processor was designed for word processing itself can be a disadvantage. You are limited to word processing jobs.

- If you need the capabilities of a computer, you'll have to buy one, since very few word processors have extensive facilities for computer-type work.

- Most manufacturers offer means of expanding or upgrading their systems, but this is within a certain framework. You are limited to their disks, printers, etc.

To sum up, what you gain in having a powerful, easy-to-use word processor, you lose in flexibility.

Computer-based systems

You should think of computer-based systems if you already have a computer, or need combined computer and word processing facilities.

- If you already have a computer, it may not be financially worthwhile buying a word processor. Work processing software for use on computers costs much less than a word processor.

- Virtually all computers have word processing software available, from the smallest microcomputer to the largest expensive machines.

- Some computer manufacturers provide special hardware/software combinations, with word processing as a primary consideration.

- You can use the computer for all non-WP jobs. As well, you can use documents created by the word processor in other contexts. For example, both an invoicing system (computer) and list processing (WP) can share the name and address list.

- A computer usually has more memory and disk space available, so longer — and more — documents can be stored and processed.

However,

- A computer is a general-purpose machine, not fixed to any one task. Hence, compromises have been made in its design, in favour of computer-type work, not word processing.

- This compromise results in a general-purpose keyboard, with general-purpose keys. There could be redundant keys (which you would never use), or keys whose label is different from their function.

- The software may not be easy to use — you may need to memorize many codes and combinations of keys. This is particularly true on small computers.

- The display could be unattractive: on many of the smaller computers, the screen will not show true descenders (the part of a letter that appears below the baseline; e.g. q, p, j, g, etc.).

Configurations

Dedicated word processors are available in three configurations: standalone, shared resources and shared logic. What does *configuration* mean?

- **Configuration** is a general term given to the arrangement of separate units within a system.

Standalone

This is the most popular configuration for small installations. It is also the least expensive of the three.

- **Standalone** means self-contained: all the units that belong to a word processor (disks, screen, keyboard) are housed in one enclosure. Usually, the printer is a separate unit, connected to the screen by a cable.

- Only one person at a time can work at a standalone system; however, if the system has foreground/background capabilities, it can be doing more than one job.

- Standalone does not necessarily mean alienated — via a suitable communications link, the machine can be connected to other word processors, computers, etc.

Shared resources/Networking

Occasionally, in small installations, a second workstation may be needed, because of large workloads. Two workstations with two printers is not always the best answer, since a printer can be shared between the machines.

- When a resource, such as a printer, is shared between two or more workstations, the configuration is called **shared resources** or **networking**.

This means that two or more screens can be doing different jobs, and using the printer only when needed.

Each workstation can communicate with other equipment (if it has communications), and none of its standalone capabilities is impaired.

Most manufacturers offer an upgrade from standalone to shared resources.

Shared logic

Consider a very large installation, with many workstations. You may think that the only solution is to have as many standalone units as needed, with perhaps some resource sharing.

There are disadvantages to this approach:
- The cost of many standalone units will be high.
- Only every two or so workstations can share resources. Consequently, many printers would be needed, many of which would be redundant.
- Total text storage capacity would be small.
- Sharing text among the workstations would be difficult, and severely restricted.

Shared logic systems solve all these problems.

- Standalone workstations are stripped of their disks, printers and control electronics. All that remain are a screen and keyboard.

- These modified workstations are connected to one electronic control and disk unit. This combined unit is often called a *Central Processing Unit* (CPU).

- A few printers are also connected to the CPU.
- The disk is not based on floppies, but on large, hard disks, with a total capacity ranging from at least 10M up to around 80M.
- Each workstation still has all the text entry, editing, printing, and storage facilities, except that these have been centralized in one CPU.
- Workstations can all share text, since only one big disk stores all the text.
- Printers can also be shared among the workstations, since they are connected to the CPU.

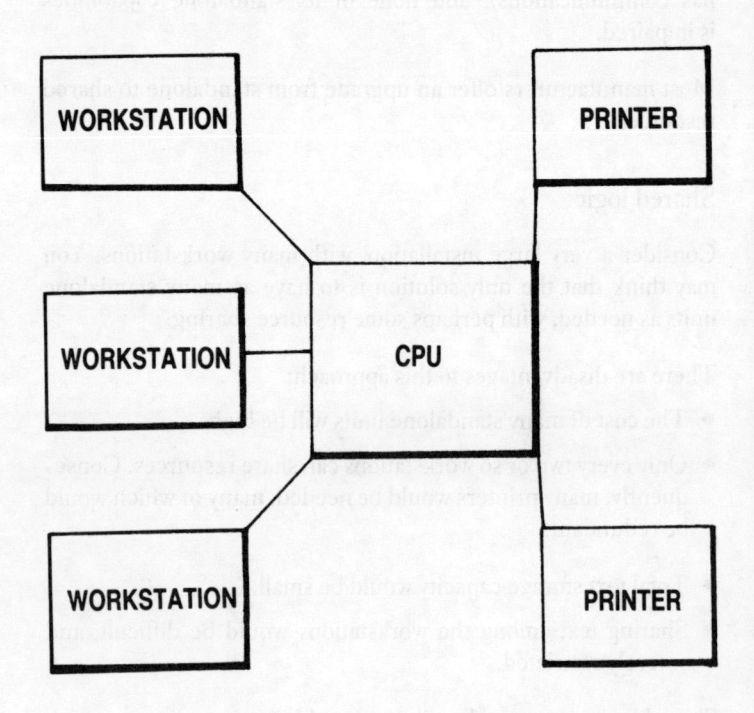

```
WORKSTATION                    PRINTER


WORKSTATION      CPU


WORKSTATION                    PRINTER
```

- For a large number of workstations, a shared logic system is cheaper than the equivalent number of standalone systems.
- More workstations can be added as needed. The maximum number that can be connected varies among manufacturers, but is somewhere between 16 and 64.

70 Word Processing

There is only one serious disadvantage to this arrangement: if the CPU breaks down, every workstation is out of action.

Despite the cost savings over standalone systems, shared logic systems are very expensive.

Sometimes, the term **shared facilities** is used to describe both shared resource and shared logic configurations.

Computer-based configurations

The configurations for computer-based word processing systems are similar to those for dedicated systems. The configuration depends on the computer.

- If you have a computer that can be used by several people at the same time (multi-user), the word processing is identical to shared logic.

- If you have one computer, used by one person at a time, it's the same as standalone.

- It is sometimes difficult to distinguish between a shared logic and shared resource configuration on a computer. Most computers that can share resources are of the shared logic variety.

Financing

One other area that can cause problems is the financing of word processing systems. There are several ways to buy systems, and the one you choose depends on many factors. Here are a few points to bear in mind:

- make use of any allowances against corporation tax that may be available;

- predict your future needs, and assess how you might want to upgrade the system;

- get advice from various finance houses, which are generally attached to merchant or clearing banks — it pays to shop around and compare rates;

- remember that there are very few second-hand machines on the market, since most people keep theirs for a long time.

There are five ways you can get a system: outright purchase, leasing, hire-purchase, bank loan and rental.

Outright purchase

- Easiest — the system is yours with minimum paperwork, and is an asset.

- You might find something better to do with the money, unless there is an immediate benefit.

Leasing

- The equipment is neither an asset nor a liability, and doesn't appear on the balance sheet.

- You can claim the full monthly payments against tax.

- Make sure you deal with a company experienced in computers or word processing, as it will be more helpful.

Hire-purchase

- Also called *lease-purchase*, it offers the same facilities as leasing.

- The equipment becomes yours at the end of the payment period.

- Interest rates could be a little higher than those for leasing.

- A down-payment or deposit is usually required.

Bank loan

- Check if there are any schemes available from the bank. If so, interest rates could be lower, and a loan could be comparatively easy to get.

Rental

- A few manufacturers or suppliers offer rental as an alternative to purchase. There is usually a mimimum period for which you must rent.

- Monthly rental payments are usually calculated as a percentage of the system value. If you work it out over a year, you'll find that it may be cheaper to buy a system.

Consult you accountant before you decide — there may be significant differences in the way each method affects your tax position, especially with regard to capital allowances.

Whatever method you choose, there are a few more things to remember:

- ask about discounts for cash with order, or buying several systems at the same time;

- demonstration machines, if they're sold, could be cheaper than brand-new ones;

- some manufacturers have their own finance companies, so rates could be better;

- ask about maintenance, as this could vary according to the method of purchase (the principal requirement for regular servicing is in the moving parts — disk drives, printers etc.);

- manufacturers tend to pitch high prices for maintenance contracts (10–12% of purchase price), even though a good machine should need little servicing. The cost of maintenance may be a major consideration in your choice. Investigate alternative methods of servicing, particularly in association with breakdown policies offered by various insurance companies. You may find you save a lot of money.

Bureaux

A word processing bureau is like the local photo-copying shop: its purpose is to allow sharing of an expensive resource among many people.

Bureaux can be independent companies, or be backed by WP manufacturers or other corporations.

A word processing bureau can provide you with a large range of services. For example:

- One-off jobs, like letters, reports, resumés, etc.

- Regular jobs, such as mail shots, reminders, etc. The names and addresses are permanently stored.

- Overload work, supplementing your system during emergencies or peak periods.

- Seminars, introducing word processing and its usefulness.

- Consulting services, in which the people running the bureau offer advice based on substantial experience and a large range of applications in word processing.

- Some bureaux offer a local sales outlet and demonstration centre.

- Coupled with sales, bureaux offer a source of supplies (disks, ribbons, etc.) as well as training and after-sales support.

- Some word processing bureaux double up as computer bureaux, providing services such as payroll, or telex facilities.

- Recruitment — some bureaux can recruit experienced operators for you, and because of their knowledge can select the best person better than recruitment agencies.

There is quite a lot to be said for using a bureau:

- Experience in word processing is readily available.
- No capital outlay required.
- A smooth and less complicated approach to word processing.
- Negotiable charges for very large or small jobs.
- Generally low charges for the work done.

Remember, though, that if you expect to use a bureau a lot, it may be financially worthwhile to get your own system.

The competition among bureaux is generally fierce, with each bureau having its favourite system. Remember also that standard charges apply only to some types of work, like mail shots. Most bureaux will want to see your job before giving a charge.

With decreasing hardware/software costs, bureaux are becoming a less attractive alternative. It may make sense to use a bureau for more complicated jobs only.

5 Evaluating systems

The hardware

One of the most important decisions to make when selecting hardware is whether to have dedicated keys or mnemonics on the keyboard. Remember:

- a system with dedicated keys means each main task of word processing has its own key; the result is a rather cluttered keyboard.

- a system using mnemonics has a simpler keyboard, but whoever uses the machine will have to remember a lot of codes.

The screen and keyboard are best judged by the person who will use the machine most. Here are a few things to check:

- remember that a detachable QWERTY keyboard will be offered on most word processors. If you need a different keyboard, you may have to look further;

- a numeric keypad is useful if you expect to work a lot with numbers;

- the screen should have at least adjustable brightness — adjustable contrast, swivel and tilt are also nice to have;

- the text on the screen should be crisp and clear, not fuzzy around the edges. It should be properly focused, stable and large enough to see comfortably.

With disks, it is important to check their storage capacities. Storage is specified in many loose ways. It's important you know the differences.

Most standalone word processors will have two disk drives. If you only find one, check how disk duplicates are made.

Evaluating systems 75

The printer is an important part of the word processing system.

- It will usually be a daisywheel printer. Dot matrix printers are an optional extra, if available at all.

- There is a large range of daisywheels to choose from. If you have an out-of-the-ordinary application, check the availability of daisywheels.

Printer speed is another abused specification. Speeds are defined in 'characters per second' (CPS), 'lines per minute' (LPM) or 'words per minute' (WPM).

- The correct (precise) unit of measurement is 'characters per second'. Other measures are difficult to compare.

- To define LPM or WPM, you have to define what a line or what a word is. Here again, most manufacturers exaggerate the practical performance of their systems.

- Bear in mind that even CPS is a nominal figure, and in practice the speed will be somewhat less.

Ribbons should in most cases be freely available from other suppliers. If you need special paper-handling equipment, remember that:

- tractor and single-sheet feeds are optional extras, and in the case of the latter are very expensive;

- disk storage capacity is expressed in 'pages', 'characters' or 'K'.

- K (Kilobytes) is the internationally agreed and correct unit of measurement — all others are manufacturer's preferences.

- Although a *byte* is the same as a *character*, remember that a K is 1024 bytes; if storage is defined in characters, the figure has usually been rounded up or down.

- Beware of capacity expressed in pages, as this is a very misleading definition. Many manufacturers consider a page to be single-spaced, in 12 pitch. This may not be your definition of a page. Remember that all capacities expressed in pages are optimistic, and in practice they are smaller.

The second important thing is to check what type of disks are used, and where they come from.

- Avoid, if you can, those systems in which only the manufacturer's disks can be used. These disks will probably be quite expensive. However, many manufacturers are becoming competitive in their pricing.

- The disks used on your WP may be specially formatted for the WP in such a way as to hinder you using any but the manufacturer's own disks. However, independent suppliers often find ways round this problem, and you should try to find such suppliers, as their disks are just as good, and usually considerably cheaper.

- Don't forget that double-sided, double-density disks will be expensive no matter where they come from.

- Any special stationery you may need to use must fit the printer or other attachments.

You may want to ask about an **acoustic hood**. This is simply a box which fits around the printer, and deadens some of the noise it makes. It is available for most makes of printers.

Finally, you should consider these two things, if they apply to you.

- What communications options are available?
- Is it possible to upgrade from standalone to shared resources or shared logic?

The software

Software is an integral part of a dedicated word processor — you don't have any choices.

One of the most important aspects of the software is the size of the unit of text it handles.

- Generally, the larger the unit, the easier it is to use the system. Size is usually expressed in thousands of characters.

Once you have clearly defined your applications, consider first any adjuncts that the software may have. These are:

- The calculator — check the accuracy of all calculations. Also check the largest numbers you can work with, and how many places after the decimal point are allowed.

- List processing — this is really a standard part of most word processors.

- Foreign languages — remember that the further a language is from Latin, the more difficult it will be to create text in it. Ask about foreign-language keyboards, daisywheels and spelling dictionaries.

- Equations — most software caters for standard mathematical symbols and the Greek alphabet.

- Records management — check the number and types of field, the maximum length of records, and what conditional selection facilities are present.

- User programming — check what this term means; grouping several keystrokes and assigning them to one key is also becoming a standard feature of word processing.

The rest of the software should be evaluated in the context of your application. The features described previously are common to most machines. The value of one machine over another is the ease with which they process your work.

You must ask these two important questions:

- What sort of message does the system give if something absurd is done? Check this by not putting a disk in the drive when you are about to save text, for example. If a message such as ERROR 39 (for example) appears, ask to see the list explaining error messages.

- How are units of text identified on disk? If you expect to process a lot of documents, easy and sensible naming conventions will help you with overall organization of text and disks.

Finally, you've seen what foreground/background and a print queue can do to ease word processing. For really large workloads, you'll need such a facility, but be prepared to pay more for a machine with it.

The supplier

Competition among suppliers and manufacturers of word processing equipment is fierce. Everyone will try to convince you that their system is best. Usually, choice of supplier follows from choice of equipment. Nevertheless, evaluating a supplier and its services is as important as the equipment.

The sales pitch

Most representatives have a very good product knowledge, and are committed to their equipment. They are also very well trained to recognize certain reactions in you, and to act on them. Obviously, they must be able to extract an order from you. Whether they do or not depends on:

- how the presentation is set up — are prices and brochures to hand, and manuals on show?

- the appearance of the representative, his or her punctuality and interest in you as a customer;

- the quality of the demonstration — is it conducted smoothly and confidently, in simple and slow English?

- the representative's honesty — are the services of the company and features of the equipment accurately represented?

Demonstrations

The demonstration of the equipment is the most important part of the sales pitch. Keep these things in mind when you go to one.

- Demonstrations are based on 'model' situations. The examples chosen are easy to show and explain.

- Demonstrations will always highlight what the equipment is best at. There are always some things it can't do well, if at all.

- You must be satisfied that the equipment will handle your work. Make sure you take a sample of your work with you, and see it being done on the machine.

- Avoid being impressed by irrelevant features of the machine. For instance, if you're a solicitor, mathematical equations are probably of no use to you.

Evaluating systems 79

- Make notes of criticisms and questions as you go along — it's easy to forget them during the course of the demonstration.

- Try to watch the machine's operator — see how things are done, the commands used, etc. Ask for a repetition if things are not clear.

Other things to remember:

- Beware if a representative criticises rival companies or their machines. It's highly unprofessional to do so. However, if you're pointed out a fact of one system you didn't know about, it pays to check it out.

- Carefully check all claims about performance and features. Question statements such as 'very easy', 'very powerful', etc.

- Question substantial discounts and other price reductions, if you're offered them, and any 'free' items.

Determine the exact level of after-sales support given. Ask at least these two questions:

- is there a 'hot line' that you can ring and ask about procedures, and get help with problems?

- will an exchange machine be given, or other arrangements made, should your system break down and take a long time to fix?

Of course, there are warranty periods, maintenance contracts, training and delivery times to check out. Check these particularly, and if necessary have them confirmed in writing before buying. Manufacturers sometimes try to get you to sign a maintenance contract as soon as your machine is installed — although as a matter of course, and statutory right, for a certain period the manufacturer should guarantee the machine against malfunctioning, whether or not a formal warranty is offered.

Finally,

- Get as much as possible in writing. This will avoid any misunderstandings.

- Don't go to any foreign supplier — you'll end up with more problems than any price difference could offset.

- All sales literature is oversimplified. You need to see the machine put through its paces, and record all positive and negative aspects.

- Try to be as knowledgeable and independent as you can.

Agreements

An agreement between you and the supplier will take the form of an order and delivery statement. It should state:

- delivery times, and charges if applicable;
- cost itemization, down-payments, etc.;
- what is being bought, with serial numbers;
- what is not included in the price (accessories, maintenance contracts, etc.);
- warranties and replacement/repair policies.

Software is included in the price of most systems. A notable exception is IBM, who have a policy of not selling you software. Instead, you pay a licence fee.

- A licence means that you can use the software as much as you like, but it is not yours.

- A licence fee may be a one-off charge, or a monthly or yearly charge, depending on the manufacturer.

From time to time, software is updated — revisions are made, or things added. You should receive these updates, but:

- make sure that any charges for the updates are specified in the agreement.

6 Implementation

Installation

Remember that the word processor will work anywhere and under any conditions you work in.

- Keep the unit away from background light, to minimize reflections on the screen.
- Ensure there is enough light to see.
- If possible, keep contrast between walls, table, etc. and the screen to a minimum.
- Don't connect the word processor on the same power line as plant, large machinery, photocopiers, fluorescent lights, etc.
- Avoid locations with extremes of temperature, dust and humidity.
- Make sure cables and power cords are not hanging loose, or in the way of feet.
- Keep away from sources of noise.
- Make sure the table, chair, keyboard and screen are at a comfortable height.
- Make sure there is plenty of room around the word processor and work area.

Training

Before you use your word processor, you must know how to use it properly and efficiently. Even if you're familiar with word processors or computers, you must still find out your system's peculiarities.

There are three main ways you can get trained: by the supplier, by an outside organization, or teach-yourself.

By your supplier

This is the most common way to get trained.

- Training sessions last from half a day to a week.
- Training may be done at your site, or at the supplier's base.
- If you are already experienced in word processors or computers, you can skip some parts.
- Training may be **bundled** (included in the price of the system) or **unbundled** (you have to pay extra).
- Don't forget to check how many people can be included in a standard training programme.
- Get a quotation in writing, stating the amount of free training, and the costs for any additional time.

By an outside organization

This is not a common way to get trained, although there are companies supplementing the training given by suppliers. Such training can be quite expensive, and the company must obviously be familiar with your equipment.

Teach-yourself

Some suppliers eliminate training altogether, to keep prices low. Instead, they give you training disks and manuals, for you to teach yourself.

- Make sure the documentation is understandable and complete.
- You should have disks, manuals for each major function available, summaries and indexes, together with installation and problem-solving manuals, and a reference card summarizing major points. If any of these are missing, you'll have problems.

Additionally, some form of assistance via the phone should be available. If you find it really hard going, the supplier will train you, for a fee.

Implementation 83

Training should cover all these things:

- proper operation of the keyboard, screen, disks, printer and any accessories;

- proper use of media (disks, ribbons, paper, etc.);

- entry, editing, printing and storage of text, and any extras, such as records management;

- other procedures, such as cleaning, care of disks, duplication of text, and what to do if something goes wrong.

Use

Here are a few day-to-day things to bear in mind when using the word processor.

The care of the word processor

- Follow the manufacturer's recommendations for cleaning the outside of the machine.

- Don't eat, drink, or smoke near the equipment.

- Don't bash the keys, or you'll get keyboard bounce, which will mean a new keyboard eventually.

- When the machine is not being used, cover it with a hood. This will prevent dust settling on it.

- If moving the machine, make sure it is disconnected from the power outlet, printer, etc.

The care of disks

Floppy disks

- ALWAYS keep floppies in their wallets. They are anti-static, and prevent contamination by dust.

- NEVER bend, fold or otherwise manipulate disks.

- NEVER touch any of the exposed areas of the disk. You may lose all the text if you do.

- NEVER put disks on top of the screen, printer, power cables, telephones or other sources of magnetism.

- NEVER force a disk into a drive, or into its wallet.

- DON'T stack disks in a vertical pile. Keep them upright, in a box.

- NEVER write on the disk envelope. Write on a label first, then stick it on the disk.

- Make sure every disk is labelled correctly.

- DON'T leave disks lying in the sun or near heaters or fridges, and keep them away from food, drink, and smoke.

- ALWAYS duplicate the disk's contents.

Drives

- NEVER open the drive door when the disk is being used. You will almost certainly lose text if you do. (Usually, a little red light glows when the drive is working.)

- DON'T put anything except a disk into the drive.

- Follow the manufacturer's recommendation for cleaning the recording head. (Usually, this is part of preventive maintenance.)

Hints and tips

A consistent and streamlined approach to word processing is vital, or you'll get no benefit from using a word processor.

If you haven't already done so, think about these issues:

- Do you have a 'house style' for producing documents? House style includes consistent terminology, consistent use of capitals, underlining and document numbering.

- Do you know how you will name and index your documents? Will you use codes, or other, fuller descriptions? How will you label the disks?

Word processors attract a lot of work, from many sources. Order and discipline are important. Don't abuse a word processor's capabilities.

NO!!!

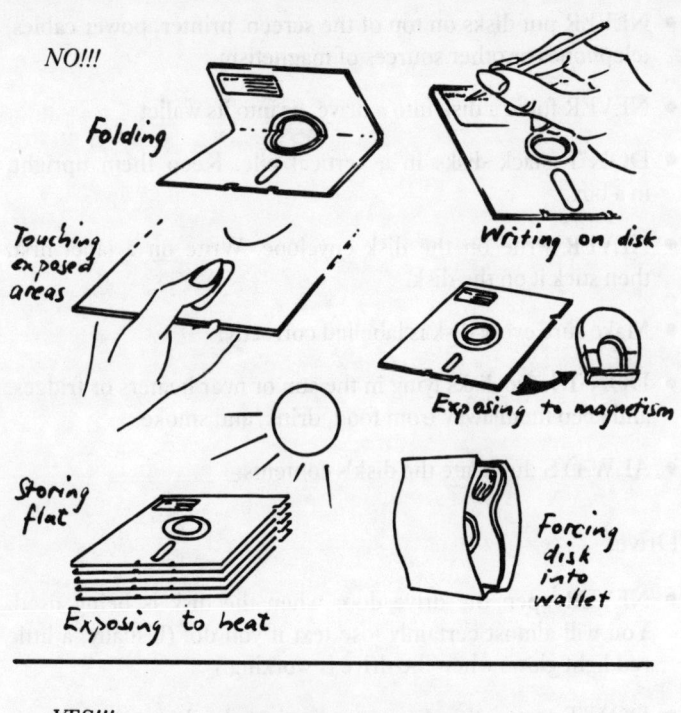

- Folding
- Touching exposed areas
- Writing on disk
- Exposing to magnetism
- Storing flat
- Exposing to heat
- Forcing disk into wallet

YES!!!

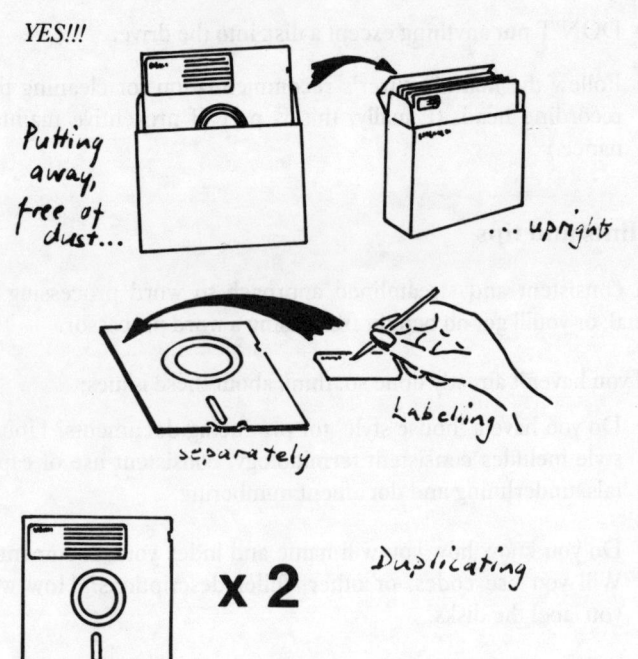

- Putting away, free of dust...
- ...upright
- Labelling separately
- Duplicating × 2

86 Word Processing

- Just because a word processor allows easy editing, don't constantly rewrite text. Plan it beforehand.

- Just because a word processor is fast, don't leave everything to the last minute. If you can, schedule the work.

- Just because word processors process text, don't use them for everything. There are still things that can be done better and quicker by hand.

In larger installations, you might consider having a 'procedures' manual, to be used by all authors and operators.

Here are a few things that are often neglected.

- Save carbon ribbons for the final draft of the text, as they are short-lived and expensive. Use fibre ribbons for routine work.

- If you use pre-printed stationery, make sure you have stock on hand, and order well in advance. Keep a set of spare daisy-wheels and ribbons.

- Characters on daisywheels get clogged up when used with fibre ribbons. Make sure they are periodically cleaned.

- Don't leave tractor or single-sheet feeds running unattended. Paper can slip out of the sprocket holes, and single-sheet feeders jam, or the paper gets out of alignment.

- Before inserting a ream of paper in a single-sheet feed, fan it. Otherwise, you may find several sheets being fed together, resulting in a jam.

If something goes wrong

Although word processing systems are very reliable, you'll probably have something go wrong at some time.

Two common causes of breakdowns are:
- loose connections;
- failure of some electronic component.

Before suspecting anything,
- check fuses in the equipment;

- check the power cords and connecting cables;
- consult troubleshooting charts in your manuals;
- check your power supply.

Word processors are not immune to fluctuations in the power supply. The supply fluctuates if another piece of equipment, on the same circuit, is switched on. The machine will probably 'hang' (stop working), and you'll have to switch off and start again.

Also remember:

- DON'T attempt to fix any electronic or mechanical component unless you know exactly what to do. Make sure you won't invalidate the warranty or maintenance contract by doing any repairs.

- You'll probably not notice any gradual deterioration in performance — the machine just goes wrong.

Disks and disk drives are another source of trouble. You'll usually be notified of any problem by a message on the screen when you try to save or recall text.

Typical reasons for disk problems are:

- the disk is not inserted properly;
- the disk drive door is open, or ajar;
- the disk has not been initialized;
- the disk has been damaged in some way;
- the disk has dust or other particles on it;
- the disk cannot rotate freely in its envelope;
- a part of the text on the disk has been erased.

The last condition is sometimes called **corruption**, and occurs if:

- the disk has been exposed to a magnetic field;
- the recording head in the drive has 'hiccoughed' and stored nonsense on the disk.

If the disk is corrupted, there is usually little you can do to recover the remaining text, so you'll have to re-initialize, thereby erasing all the text.

88 Word Processing

Before giving up the disk, open the drive door and jiggle the disk — sometimes this aligns it a bit better in the drive — and try again. Also check the freedom of movement in the envelope, by rotating the disk with your fingers through the hub, but be careful.

If nothing seems to work, get your duplicate and use that.

One final problem you may get with drives is oxide build-up on the recording head. Oxide builds up because the head is in direct contact with the disk. Friction causes some of the magnetic compound to be rubbed off. Head-cleaning is a part of preventive maintenance, and should be done when the engineer pays his regular service call.

With printers:

- check that the daisywheel and ribbon are securely positioned;
- check that any attachments are correctly in place;
- check that the printer's cover is firmly closed.

Finally, it's a good idea to keep a log of:

- date, time and symptom of problem;
- what the problem turned out to be;
- what was fixed, and when.

This will help you identify similar problems, should they recur.

Preserving the investment

Insurance

Word processing systems are still quite expensive, so it pays to have adequate insurance cover on them.

- If you are using one in the office, you could increase the value of the office equipment policy.

- In the home, it could be covered by a home-and-contents-type policy.

- If your livelihood depends on it, see about loss-of-profits cover. If you have a lot of valuable text stored, ask about recreation of records, should the text be destroyed.

Implementation 89

- Get breakdown included in your insurance cover. This usually covers non-wear-and-tear repair costs above a specified minimum (e.g. £50 per call).

Maintenance contracts

Maintenance contracts are offered by all word processing suppliers. It can be useful to take one out, because if you don't:

- you will be treated with the lowest priority when a problem arises;
- you have to pay for every hour the engineer is at your site;
- you will have to pay for all replacement and repairs, which in the case of electronic faults will be very expensive.

Before signing a contract, check the following:

- What services are provided, and at what times?
- Where are the services carried out — on site or at base?
- What are your obligations as a customer?
- What is the response time — i.e. how long before an engineer arrives?
- If it is a major problem, will you be given a replacement machine?
- What items are excluded from maintenance?

Before you decide whether to sign, assess probabilities. Average maintenance rates are between 10% and 12% of the purchase price per year. That covers a lot of breakdown and maintenance, which a good machine should not require. It might still be cheaper to pay for each breakdown separately as necessary.

Also, check how the manufacturer charges replaced parts. Certain items that may need replacing — e.g. memory boards — can easily be repaired, and should not be charged at full purchase price if replaced.

Finally make sure you pay maintenance only on the hardware/software value of the system (you don't want to pay maintenance on training, if this is an additional charge).

7 Glossary

Acoustic hood: a box that covers a printer and deadens some of the noise it makes.

Acronym: a word formed from the first letters, or first few letters, of several other words. **Spool** is an acronym for **simultaneous peripheral operation on line**.

Algorithm: the procedural steps for the solution of a specific problem. A simple example is a food recipe.

Alphanumeric: a type of *field* within a *record* that can hold letters or numbers. Also describes a *character* that can be a numeral or a letter of the alphabet.

Automatic repeat: a feature of word processor *keyboards* in which a character is automatically repeated if its key is held down. This saves you repeatedly pressing the key.

Background: a part of a word processor that takes care of work not needing your attention. For example, printing can be done in background, which leaves you free to enter or edit text. Cf. **Foreground**.

Backspace: (n) a key which, when pressed, makes the *cursor* move one position to the left. This key is used to correct simple typing mistakes on a line of text. (v) to use the backspace key to correct mistakes.

Bidirectional: describes a printer that prints both when the printing mechanism moves to the right and when it returns.

Block: (n) a group of words, lines or paragraphs which is treated as one unit by the word processor. See also **Move, Copy, Mark**.

Boilerplates: standard paragraphs or other data held on file for use in different documents.

Bold: a way of producing text in which each character is darker and thicker than normal.

Buffer: the name given to the part of the word processor's *memory* that holds text.

Bundled: describes a system in which everything is included in one price. Cf. **Unbundled**.

Bureau: a company that provides the services of a word processor and expertise to people who don't have a word processor.

Carbon ribbon: a printer made of thin plastic coated with carbon. It gives a very high quality appearance, but is expensive and doesn't last very long. Cf. **Fibre ribbon**.

Carriage return: a key used to mark the end of a line or paragraph of text. Often just called **Return**.

Cartridge disk: a large, high-capacity *disk* housed in a round plastic cartridge.

Cartridge ribbon: a printer ribbon which is contained in a plastic cartridge. This makes it easily removed and replaced.

Centering: putting a line of text, such as a heading, in the middle of the screen or paper, between the *margin* settings.

Character: a letter of the alphabet, a numeral or a special symbol, such as ?,), £.

Character formation: the way a character is displayed on a screen or printed on paper. On the screen, a character is made up of tiny dots of light. On paper, it is fully formed — i.e. not made up of dots. See also **Dot matrix, Daisywheel**.

Character set: the total number of characters that can be displayed on a screen or printed on paper.

Code: a system in which letters, numbers or other symbols are arbitrarily assigned a meaning.

Communications: an additional unit of *hardware*, which when coupled with some *software*, enables a word processor to exchange text or other information with other equipment, such as telexes, or other word processors.

Computer: a general-purpose electronic machine for processing information; also forms the basis of a word processor.

Configuration: general term given to the arrangement of physical units within a system.

Copy (Block): a procedure to move a block of text from one location to another within the text. The block is not *deleted* from its original position. Cf. **Move**.

Corruption: the inadvertent destruction of text on a disk, by exposure to stray magnetic fields.

CPI: acronym for *characters per inch*, a measure of printing *pitch*.

CPS: acronym for *characters per second*, a measure of printing speed.

CR: an acronym for *carriage return*, found more often on computer keyboards than on word processor keyboards.

CRT: acronym for *cathode ray tube*, the correct technical name for the word processor screen.

Cursor: a flashing or stationary rectangle or thin line of light, used to indicate where text is to be entered or changed.

Cursor control keys: a set of four or more keys, with arrows on them. The arrows indicate the direction in which the cursor will move if the key is pressed. The four directions are up, down, left and right. An optional fifth key takes the cursor to the top left-hand side of the screen.

Glossary 93

Cut-and-paste: general name given to the task of moving pieces of text from one position to another.

Daisywheel: (1) a circular disk with protruding spokes, resembling a flower with petals. At the tip of each spoke is a character. (2) the name given to a printer that uses daisywheels: the wheel rotates until the right character is in position, and a hammer flies out and hits it on to paper.

Decimal tab: a key used for entering numbers, to save you worrying about the alignment of decimal points. Pressing the key moves the cursor to the decimal point, and the cursor then moves from right to left until the 'point' key is pressed.

Dedicated: set apart, assigned or exclusively reserved for one purpose. A *dedicated word processor* can only do word processing, nothing else.

Default: the name given to a value, such as a margin setting, that the word processor automatically assumes, in the absence of any entries from you.

Delete: to remove or eliminate a part of text, such as a word or a line. Text can also be deleted from a disk.

Descender: the part of a letter that appears below a baseline; e.g. *q, y, p, g, j*.

Dictionary: a collection of short pieces of text, stored on disk, which is reserved for special applications, e.g. a disk-based spelling dictionary. The same as a **library**.

Discretionary hyphen: a hyphen that is inserted between words to improve the appearance of text. A discretionary hyphen is not permanent: if the length of a line is changed, the hyphen may be automatically dropped by the system. Cf. **Required hyphen**.

Disk: a storage device consisting of a flat circular plate, made of plastic or aluminium, coated with a magnetizable material. The disk may be *exchangeable, fixed, floppy,* or *hard*.

Disk-drive: a device consisting of a motor and an electromagnet which enables text to be stored on disks. The motor spins the disk while the recording head moves over the surface of the disk, recording text.

Display format: the amount of characters that can fit on the screen, described as either the number of lines and characters per line, or the total number of characters.

Document: a portion of text treated by the word processor as one complete unit.

Document assembly: the procedure of collating separate sections of text, such as paragraphs, to form a new, complete document.

Document recovery: a facility on some word processors to re-establish a document which has been accidentally deleted.

Dot matrix: name given to a type of printer that prints characters as a set of fine dots within a grid of rows and columns, called a *matrix*.

Duplicate: to make a copy of either a document on a disk, or the contents of the whole disk, on to another disk.

Editing: changing and revising text, involving substitutions, corrections, deletions and insertions.

Elite: name of a printing *pitch* in which 12 characters are printed to the horizontal inch.

Emboldening: a procedure whereby the word processor prints text in **bold**.

Emulation: an aspect of *communications*, in which the word processor — to make the connection to another piece of equipment easier — 'pretends' it is a common computer terminal.

Error detection: a feature built into *communications* to ensure that any text that has been sent to, or received from another device has not been distorted during its transmission.

Exchangeable disk: a disk that can be removed from the disk drive. Using exchangeable disks means that more than one disk

Glossary 95

can be used to store text. *Floppy disks* are exchangeable. Cf. **Fixed disks**.

Fibre ribbon: a ribbon made of textile or nylon, and treated with ink. Its print quality is acceptable, and it is inexpensive and lasts a long time. Cf. **Carbon ribbon**.

Field: a subdivision of a *record*, which contains only a specific type of information, e.g. in a 'name and address' record, the post code and town are both *fields*. See also **Record**.

File: an organized collection of related *records* on a disk, e.g. a set of names and addresses.

Fixed disk: a disk which cannot be removed from the disk drive, i.e. it is built-in. One disk stores all the text. *Winchesters* are fixed disks. Cf. **Exchangeable disks**.

Floppy disk: a disk made of flexible plastic, contained in a square rigid envelope, available in $5\frac{1}{4}''$ and $8''$ sizes.

Font: a set of characters of a particular style and type, e.g. Pica Cubic.

Footer (or **Footing**): a short piece of text or other information, that appears at the bottom of every page in a document.

Footnote: a piece of text which appears at the bottom of a page. It is referenced by a number, and elaborates on material contained within the main text. [N.B. Not the same as a **footer**.]

Foreground: a part of the word processor that handles text entry and editing, and any other activities which need your direct involvement. Cf. **Background**.

Format: the layout, presentation or arrangement of text on a screen or on paper.

Formatting: the process of defining areas on a disk where text is to be stored. With some word processors, you have to buy specially formatted disks, i.e. the manufacturer's own brand, unless some other supplier has succeeded in cracking the formatting code.

Function keys: extra keys found only on a word processor *keyboard*. They are used to control editing, printing, storage and other processing of text.

Glossary: a term used by some manufacturers to describe a collection of *standard paragraphs*.

Hard disk: a disk which is made of rigid material, such as aluminium. Hard disks may be *fixed* or *exchangeable*, and come in $5\frac{1}{4}''$, $8''$ and $14''$ sizes.

Hardware: all the parts of a word processor that can be seen and touched. Cf. **Software**.

Header (or **Heading**): a short piece of text or other information that appears at the top of every page in a document.

Home: name given to the top left-hand side of the screen.

Hot zone: (also called **soft zone**) an area in a line of text to the left of the right margin, of adjustable size. The word processor detects any word that starts in the hot zone, and if the word won't fit on the line, a hyphen can be inserted. Hot zones are used to tidy up the appearance of text which has been created with word **wraparound**.

Hyphen: see **Discretionary hyphen** and **Required hyphen**.

Hyphenation: the division of a word into two parts if it can't fit on one line. The first part of the word is ended with a hyphen.

Icon: a command or function represented graphically on screen. You use icons by pointing to the picture and pressing the mouse or other control.

Indent: to start text entry a number of spaces away from the left *margin*.

Index: a list of documents, automatically created by the word processor, that are held on disk. The index shows the name and size of the document, along with some other information.

Ink-jet printer: a fast, quiet, high-quality printer which prints by throwing ink on to paper at high speed.

Insert: to add characters, lines or other portions of text to existing text.

Integrated software: a suite of programs designed to function together. Usually contains at least a database, word processor and spreadsheet. You can switch easily from one to the other, and easily incorporate files or data from another program on the disk.

Interface: an aspect of *communications*, being the physical connection between (for example) a word processor and another device. The interface arranges text and controls the transmission of text between the machines.

Justification: the process of inserting tiny spaces between letters in a word, or between words themselves, to make the last letter of a line appear at the right margin. Justified text looks like a column. (This text is justified.) Cf. **Unjustified, Ragged right.**

K (or Kb): an abbreviation for **Kilobyte**, which is a unit of measurement of *memory* or disk storage capacity. It is 1024 *bytes*, or *characters*.

Key: (n) a switch on a *keyboard* labelled with a character. Pressing the key brings up the character on the screen.
(v) to enter text by pressing keys. Sometimes called *key in*.

Keyboard: a collection of switches, or *keys*, used to enter text.

Keystroke: pressing a single key on a keyboard once.

Laser printer: a very fast dot matrix printer especially useful for making print-quality copies.

Library: the same as **dictionary**.

Line ending: a special character denoting the end of a short line of text, created by pressing the *carriage return* key.

Line graphics: a feature of some word processors whereby boxes can be put around text, or other horizontal and vertical lines can be drawn.

Line spacing: the number of lines in a vertical inch of paper. Usually specified as *single*, double, *half* or *1½* spacing, but you can get even more gradations.

List processing: a feature of most word processors which allows a list of *variable* information to be created and automatically included within a standard piece of text. For example, when you are creating a list of names and addresses, together with a reminder notice: the system automatically includes the name and address in the notice, and produces a letter for each individual.

Logic-seeking: a characteristic of printers which effectively skip over any blank spaces in text, thereby achieving much faster printing speeds.

M (or Mb): like *K*, a unit of measurement of disk storage capacity, being 1,024,000 *bytes* or *characters*, i.e. 1000K.

Margin: the physical boundary of text, on the left and right side of a screen or page.

Mark (Block): (v) to identify a specific portion of text (by putting special codes called *block markers*) at the beginning and end of the piece of text, for special editing. See also **Block, Move, Copy**.

Memory: a set of electronic components in which text is stored during entry and editing.

Merge: to combine units of text, or to append one document to another, to form a new document.

Glossary 99

Micro disk: also called a *micro floppy*. A small, high-capacity disk (ranging from 3″ to 3½″ in diameter) enclosed in a rigid outer cover.

Microprocessor: a small electronic package that controls the hardware of the word processor, under the guidance of *software*.

Mnemonic: literally, a memory aid; as applied to word processing, it is a code consisting of a few characters, which instructs the word processor to carry out a certain task.

Monospacing: a method of printing in which each character printed takes up the same amount of space horizontally, irrespective of the size of the character. Cf. **Proportional**.

Mouse: a hand-held controller device for moving a pointer or cursor about the screen. It moves on a roller ball or wheels, and has command buttons on it.

Move (Block): to remove a block from one location, and reposition it at another. The block is deleted from its original location. See also **Copy, Mark, Block**.

Multi-strike ribbon: a type of *carbon ribbon* which lasts longer than an ordinary *(single-strike)* ribbon, since it is good for several passes.

NLQ: 'near letter quality' — a term used to describe high-quality dot matrix printers. They work by striking each character several times over.

Numeric: a type of *field* or *character* that can only contain or specify a numeral. Cf. **Alphanumeric**.

Numeric keypad: a small *keyboard* which only has keys with the numerals on it.

Orphan line: the last line of a paragraph, which appears by itself at the top of a page. Cf. **Widow line**.

Package: name given to word processing *software* that is bought for use on an existing computer.

Page: the amount of text which a piece of paper holds: sometimes also describes the amount of text a screen can hold. Otherwise, any unit of text that is separated by **page breaks**.

Page break: a code which is inserted (either by the operator or by the system) during *pagination*. When the printer encounters a page break, it ejects the paper, feeds a new one in, and resumes printing. With continuous stationery, it leaves a space each side of the perforation.

Page display: name given to a *display format* in which between 50 and 70 lines of text can be displayed on the screen.

Pagination: the process of breaking up text into units that will fit on a given size of page, by inserting *page breaks*.

Part-page display: name given to a *display format* in which between 16 and 24 lines of text can be displayed on the screen. This is the most common display format in word processing systems.

Pica: name of a printing *pitch* in which 10 characters are printed to the horizontal inch.

Pitch: a measure of character spacing, i.e. the number of characters that are printed in a horizontal inch. Also measured in *characters per inch* (**CPI**). See also **Pica, Elite**.

Printer: a device that prints text received from a word processor on to paper, in conjunction with a ribbon and a *daisywheel* (or other printing element).

Programming: strictly speaking, the art and science of writing computer programs, or *software*. Also refers to the process of assigning many keys to only one key, to simplify some commonly used procedures. One keystroke thus becomes equivalent to several keystrokes.

Prompt: a cue or message issued by the word processor, to which you must react in order to have a task carried out. Also used as a verb.

Proportional: method of printing in which each character printed takes up only the space it needs, rather than a fixed amount of space as in *monospacing*, e.g. the letter *i* needs less space than *m*.

Protocol: as applied to *communications*, it is the set of rules by which the transmission and reception of text is governed.

Queue: a method of lining up documents to be printed automatically, without you having to initiate the printing of each document individually. Used in *background*.

QWERTY: internationally the most widely accepted arrangement of keys in a *keyboard*, named after the first six keys on the left of the first row of the keyboard. Another arrangement is the AZERTY.

Ragged right: name given to text that is *unjustified*, i.e. the right-hand side of the text is not straight, but ragged (the text is all pushed towards the left margin).

Recall: (v) to transfer text stored on a disk to the word processor's *memory*, so that editing or other processing can be done to it.

Record: a subdivision of a *file*, itself consisting of *fields*.

Records management: a feature of some word processing systems whereby the word processor can be used to create, edit, store, *sort* and select, and print information that is not necessarily related to text. Maintaining lists of customers and their details is an example of this kind of information.

Reformat: to change the *format* of text, involving changing margins, page lengths, printing pitch, justification, etc.

Rehyphenation: inserting or deleting hyphens in text where the line length has changed as a result of changed *margin* settings.

Rename: to change the name (or other identifier) of a document stored on disk.

Repagination: the process of changing the lengths of pages, which may be required if text has been inserted or deleted from a document. Repagination involves putting new *page breaks* into the text.

Required hyphen: a hyphen that occurs normally in a word (such as *co-educational*). A required hyphen is not removed automatically by the system during *rehyphenation*.

Ruler: a line that appears below the *status line* showing the left and right *margin* and *tab* settings.

Save: to transfer to a document from the word processor's *memory* to a disk. See also **Recall**.

Screen: the part of the word processor that displays text, similar to a television. See also **VDU, CRT**.

Scrolling: A screen can only display a limited amount of characters. To bring the other text into view, a line is removed from the top or bottom of the screen, and a new line brought in at the other end. This action is repeated continuously, giving the illusion of text moving past the screen, in the manner of a scroll.

Search and replace: a facility on word processors in which a specified *string* is searched for in the text, and when found, replaced by another string.

Shared facilities: a general term given to either *shared logic* or *shared resources configurations*.

Shared logic: a *configuration* in which a number of word processors are stripped of their disks and control electronics, and instead connected to a central, high-capacity disk unit. This central unit is called a *central processing unit,* or *CPU*.

Shared resources: a *configuration* in which a couple of word processors share a resource, such as a printer.

Single-sheet feed: an attachment to a printer basically consisting of a tray that holds a ream of paper. Under instructions

Glossary 103

from the printer, it feeds a single sheet at a time into the printer, without the operator having to do so.

Single-strike ribbon: a type of *carbon ribbon* which is only good for one pass in the printer, after which it has to be discarded. It gives the highest quality print.

Software: name given to all the programs (sets of instructions) that the *microprocessor* can act on, and thereby control the operation of the *hardware*.

Soft zone: See **Hot zone**.

Sort: to arrange or order information in a specific sequence, e.g. alphabetically.

Spool: an acronym for **s**imulataneous **p**eripheral **o**peration **o**n **l**ine; in more technical terms, the word describes how a *print queue* works.

Standalone: describes a word processor that has all the components needed for word processing enclosed in one unit; *standalone* means self-contained, not requiring any add-ons or supports.

Standard paragraph: a piece of text which can be a part of many different documents, e.g. a clause within a contract. It is stored on disk, and brought into the text when needed. A collection of standard paragraphs makes up a *library* or *glossary*, and is used in *document assembly*.

Stationery: the paper on which text is printed is of two types: *single-sheet* and *continuous*. *Single-sheet* describes the ordinary single pieces of paper, such as the standard A4. *Continuous* stationery is a continuous strip folded into sheets, and perforated at the end of each sheet. Sprocket holes on the sides enable it to pass through a *tractor feed* on top of the printer.

Status line: a line at the top or bottom of the screen that gives information about work currently being done (specifically things like the *cursor* position within the text, the length of a page, and any *prompts* the system may issue.

Stop code: a special character used to denote the position where information is to be automatically filled in at a later stage, by the system. Also called *start code* or *switch code*. See also **Variable**.

String: a sequence of adjoining characters; words are strings, as are acronyms and abbreviations.

Subscript: a character which is printed below the baseline; $_2$ is a subscript in H_2O.

Superscript: a character which is printed above the baseline; ^{3} is a superscript in x^3.

System: an interrelated collection of objects working together as a unit for a common purpose. A word processor is a system.

Systems disk: a special disk which must be inserted into the system after switching on — it carries the *software* that makes the word processor work, and the operator's first task is to transfer this into memory.

Tab: the name of a key which positions the *cursor* directly at a specified point on a line. (This saves repeatedly pressing the space bar.) The specified point is called a *tab setting*.

Text: letters, numbers, words and other symbols that make up a body of information. Pictures are generally excluded from text.

Text editor (or **Text processor**): another name for a word processor.

Text register: a special temporary storage place for *blocks* that are being copied. See also **Block, Copy**.

Thermal printer: a printer which uses special heat-sensitive paper.

Tractor feed: an attachment to a printer that feeds *continuous stationery* through, using two circular belts with protruding studs that catch the sprocket holes in the stationery.

Typeface: also called *typestyle* or *font*, it is a set of characters of a particular style and size.

Unbundled: describes a system in which the components making it up are given separate prices; the system is built by selecting the required components, and the total price is then calculated.

Underlining: a feature of word processors in which text is automatically underlined as it is entered.

Unjustified: the name given to text that has not been *justified*; the right-hand side of the text is ragged, and hence called *ragged right*. Cf. **Justification**.

Variable: a piece of information that varies from document to document, such as a name in a circular letter. Variables are stored as a list on disk. See **List processing**.

VDU: acronym for V*isual* D*isplay* U*nit*; the collective name for screen and keyboard.

Widow line: the first line of a paragraph that appears by itself at the bottom of a page. Cf. **Orphan line**.

Windowing: splitting the screen into several sections or windows, each showing different data.

Word processing: the use of a computer's features, such as its versatility, speed, compactness and cost-effectiveness, for the typing, editing, storage, printing and communication of written information.

Word processor: a machine (a computer) designed specifically to work with letters, words, paragraphs and other pieces of written information.

Workstation: name given to a *standalone* word processor, or a component of a *shared facilities* system.

WP: acronym for W*ord* P*rocessing*.

WPM: acronym for w*ords* p*er* m*inute*, a not-always-precise unit of measurement for the speed of printing.

Wraparound: a feature of word processors whereby a word that can't fit on the end of a line is automatically carried over to the next line. The operator therefore does not have to end the line manually.

WYSIWYG: acronym for 'What You See Is What You Get', i.e. the text is laid out on screen in the way it will be printed.